AF422942

UNCOMMON COURAGE

A NAVAL OFFICER IN WORLD WAR II

LINDA BAKER

This book is dedicated to Esther's family

and to the brave women and men of our armed forces.

Thank you for your service.

CONTENTS

FOREWORD

My mother showed uncommon courage in leaving her family and everything she knew, traveling halfway around the world, to serve in a war that could have ended her life.

Esther Showe joined the Navy because she loved the ocean but didn't see the Pacific until she was posted to California. She always enjoyed being near water, and Esther Williams was her favorite movie star.

Sadly, Esther passed away on December 9, 2004, so I am relying on notes she left, papers she kept, letters she wrote, and family memories to tell the story of her military service in WWII as a Naval Officer.

By studying her notes, letters home, and military orders, I mined the Internet to discover the backstories of the places where she served and the ships she sailed on.

In telling Mom's military story, it happens to be interwoven with my father's story at a certain point. My father's military service in the Navy during WWII will be a separate, more extensive story because he served in the Navy for a much longer time than my mother. Mom was in the reserves while my father enlisted in the regular Navy.

Linda Baker
March 2024

EARLY DAYS

Esther Marie Taddiken was born on the family farm on August 2, 1914, in Clay Center, Kansas. She was one of the six children of John Behrens Taddiken and Margaret Young Taddiken.

Her brothers and sisters were Mrs. Alberta Taddiken Murphy, Mrs. Lavonne Taddiken McIntosh, John Wilber Taddiken, Ervin Taddiken, and Mrs. Leona Taddiken Carson.

Esther is standing second to the right in this family photo from Clay Center, Kansas taken in the early 1940s.

Her schooling began at Washington School, a one room schoolhouse. She graduated from Clay Center County High School, Class of 1932, after which, she entered the Research College of Nursing in Kansas City, Missouri in 1933, graduating as a registered nurse in 1936.

In St. Louis, Missouri, she worked as a charge nurse from Aug. 1936 to June 1940 before becoming a private duty nurse in Moberly, Missouri, and other places in the area.

Class of 1936, Research Hospital School of Nursing

One of Esther's private duty patients was the infamous "Goat Gland Doctor," Dr. John R. Brinkley. To quote, Gerald Carson, author of *The Roguish World of Doctor Brinkley*, "Dr. Brinkley was able to focus all the fears and frustrations of growing old on his goat-gland deal, with such skill that thousands of elderly gentlemen in the Western states believed that a frisky young goat, and Brinkley, could make them again as they once were. Thousands of goats gave up their virility in this dubious cause."

In Kanas City

Mom told me that she and a friend were tired of sick people, so they enrolled for a brief time at Kansas State College of Agriculture and Applied Science in Manhattan, Kansas. She stayed with a woman offering room and board in her home. The meals they were supposed to get consisted of very watery soup.

Great Lakes Naval Base and US Naval Hospital, Mare Island, California

Esther entered the US Navy on May 2nd, 1942 as a Navy reservist. She was called to active duty on June 23rd, 1942 to Great Lakes Naval Base, Great Lakes, Illinois for a physical to determine her fitness for duty.

If she failed the physical, she could not have entered the Navy.

Mom said the doctor found spots on her lungs, so it seems passing the physical was a close thing. As far as I know, she never smoked; the spots could have come from dust. Apparently, the doctor didn't think the spots were enough to keep her out of the Navy.

After passing the physical, she became a Reserve Nurse in the Nurse Corps of the United States Navy with the rank of Ensign, her service number was 156186.

She proceeded to her active-duty station, US Naval Hospital, Mare Island, California, on June 25th, 1942.

Here is an excerpt from a letter Esther wrote to her parents regarding her trip to the Great Lakes Naval Base:

Dear Folks,

Well I hope you're O.K., if I ever see a bathtub again, I think I will faint.

I arrived at the Great Lakes Naval training center after ages, and we were run through a physical examination. There were two of us. We drove along on the elevated train for miles. I have not the faintest idea where we are now.

I left Chicago 2:00pm on the California Challenger. I have not the faintest idea where I'll end up, but they said it would probably take at least 2 days and 3 nights. I just finished breakfast the food on trains always tastes good. We had egg, ham, orange juice, milk, and toast. It cost us fifty cents.

Her first duty station in the Navy was the Mare Island Naval Base Hospital, San Diego, California. This hospital would be a major stopping point for casualties evacuated from military action in the South Pacific.

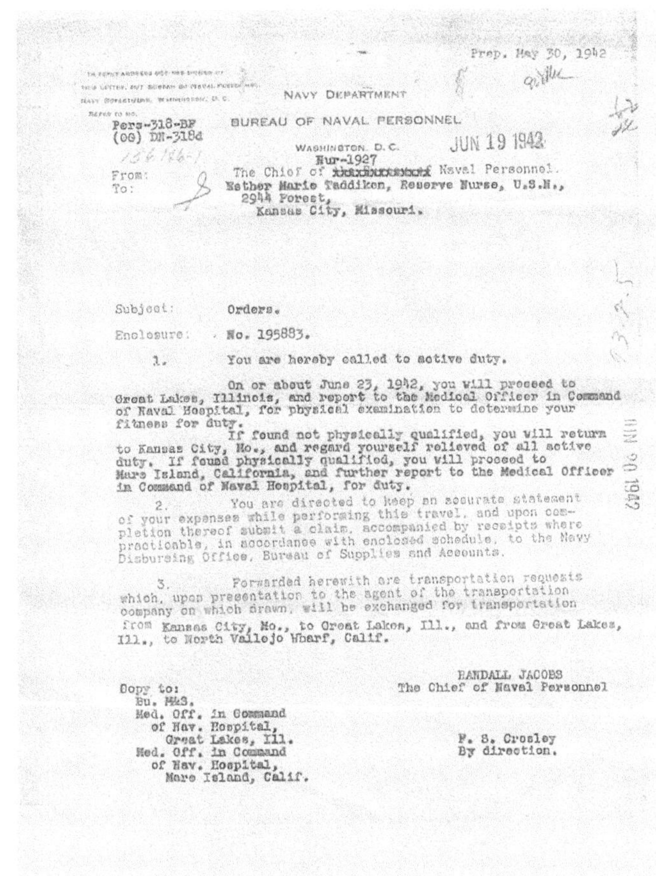

Esther's call to active duty, June 19, 1942

From her letters home, you can tell she walked into some growing pains to acclimatize new personnel to military life and establish an efficient system for taking care of patients.

This is where she met my father, Jean Showe, when he was in the US Naval Hospital at Mare Island probably for a hernia operation. Dad told the story of Mom disarming a Marine at the hospital having what we now call a post-traumatic stress disorder (PTSD) episode. Back in the day they called it, "going Asiatic." According to Dad, the Marine was threatening people with a gun, and Mom walked in and took the gun away from him.

The Marine, from Texas, kept in touch with Mom through the years. My father told me about it and Mom talked about her "little Marine."

I don't know where exactly the episode of the Asiatic (PTSD) Marine took place. Mom mentions a female Marine with psychiatric problems at Mare Island Naval Hospital in her letters home, but she did not mention where she met her "little Texas Marine." The bulk of the patients at Naval hospitals were Navy and Marine corps personnel.

Jean Showe taken in San Francisco 1943

This is the time when Mom and Dad fell in love. As she mentioned in her letters home, their love was against Navy regulations because Jean was enlisted and Esther was an officer. Her scrap book contains napkins, drink coasters, match books, and playbills from some of the top places in San Francisco and San Diego in the 1940s.

Dad said he fell in love with Mom because of her nice ways. In other words, he liked her style. They corresponded for the two years they were apart. I don't know if they knew they would both support the same military operations in the South Pacific.

There was censorship of the locations of military personnel during WWII. All personal correspondence by the military was read by censors and could be redacted by them. It seems like Esther was good at following the rules of censorship because none of her letters had any redactions by the censors.

Mom arrived at Mare Island Naval Base as the war in the Pacific was heating up. From her letters, you can sense the growing pains of the war effort. She had experience as a nurse, had been on her own, was reliable, and was very patriotic. I think all these qualities were needed and appreciated as the convoys of casualties arrived at the base hospital.

What follows are excerpts from letters Esther wrote to her parents and her sister, Alberta Taddiken Murphy, her sister Leona (Nonie) Carson, and family about her experiences at the U.S. Naval Hospital at Mare Island, California, and her experiences overseas.

My mother wrote to all her siblings and many other people, but unfortunately most of those letters have not survived. I included letters I found from her brother, John Wilber Taddiken, who was in the Army, 9th R.C.N. TR., 9th Division, A.P.O #9, and one she wrote to my father, Jean William Showe. Mom also had many aunts, uncles, and cousins. She was always concerned about her family but, in the interest of brevity, I edited most of her family and friend remarks until she was overseas.

~

July 1, 1942

I arrived safe, and sound and it is hotter than Hades. It was terrific. Everyone is very nice, and the food is excellent, but I imagine one gets used to it later on.

They put me to work this morning. What they call work, I call play. The ones or no one seems to know where anything is, you learn by the hit or miss system.

I finally ended up in Vallejo after a long trip. It is about 30 miles to San Francisco. We get every other weekend off which isn't so bad. The girls here all wear civilian clothes. I think we go into uniform later. I was measured today.

If I ever ran a place, I swear I'm going to take people and show them around. My roommate is from Ohio. She went to work today too. There is a cotton wood tree right outside my window.

Author's note: The cotton wood tree was a reminder of home in Kansas.

~

July 5, 1942

The work here isn't very hard it is mostly changing my ways because they do so differently, but I really don't mind. Would it be too much trouble to send the small radio? I will send you the amount for postage if it is too much. I would buy one out here, but if it isn't a problem to send the small radio, I would rather not. We are going to have some very nice uniforms pretty soon they are awfully cute.

My roommate has a radio, but it doesn't work so well. I fixed it so that we can get two stations now and they don't come in so very well. In Vallejo things are extraordinarily high. I guess it's due to the fact that there are so many government workers there.

July 7, 1942

Work is getting more interesting. The chief aim seems to be to pass the buck if you're good at that you would be good in the Navy. I feel so darn sorry for the kids here that I wonder some-times that they stay as sober as they do. Orinn Schli..... (don't know how to spell it) and I went to the show last night it was Eleanor Powell and Red Skeleton in "Ship Ahoy" we went on the grounds therefore it only cost us a dime.

We just had a conference and Miss Zollnan, the Chief Nurse, says we now have our rating, which is the same as an Ensign, we ordered our purses, which were $3.98, and our suits cost $40. They buy us one and I suppose I'll have to buy the rest. Our hose I suppose will have to be black which doesn't sound very alluring, but the hats are as cute as they can be. But all we need are two street uniforms and then the others and they give us six. I'm going to try to make my five last. I do hope they will.

There are two girls here from Halstead and one from the University of Kansas. There's more work here than one can shake a leg at. We taught the new corpsmen to make beds this morning. You should see them they are so cute. Big clumsy things from the farms and all over. One had a birthday today and no one congratulated him on the occasion I felt truly sorry for him. Another had leave over the weekend, got drunk, and got married. I don't know whether he regretted it or not. I must close now and see what else I can find out about the joint, something new comes up every day.

L to R: Martha Comfort, Esther Taddiken, Helen Orinin at Mare Island Naval Base Hospital, November 1942

July 17, 1942

Today has been rather a hard day. Thanks for all the publicity; my scrapbook grows bigger and bigger. We worked like the dickens today and yesterday. Today was inspection and the captain looked at the bed springs so now the boys don't get leave, because they were dirty. It's a darn shame because those boys really worked hard all week. He suspended it for a whole week. No shows or anything. I think he's an old crab, but there doesn't seem to be anything anyone can do about it.

We had a second typhoid shot. Mine came out the same as before. My roommate's got all red but so far, my arm is a little red. You should see the picture on my pass. I'm going to mark over it.

July 24, 1942

We are working hard. I'm sorry I won't be home for the picnic but I'm in the Navy and how.

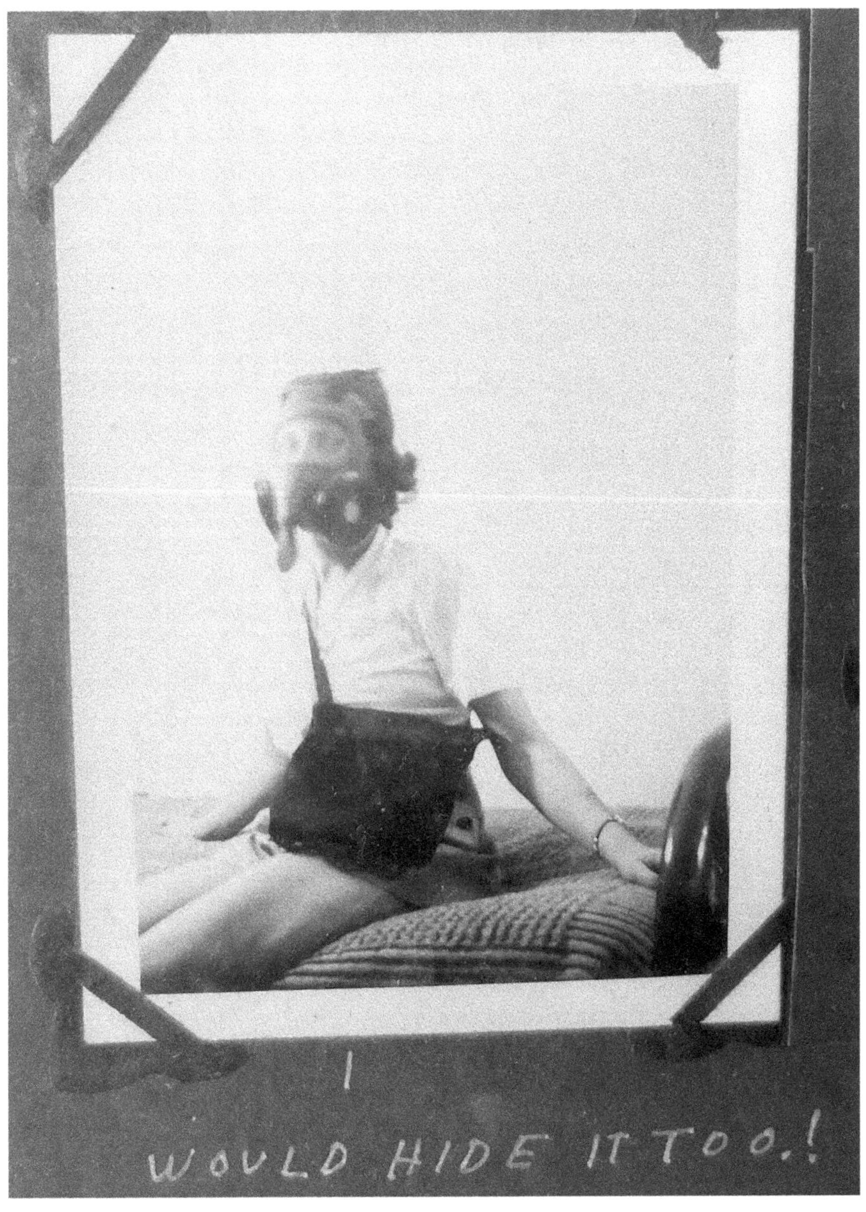

We have now had our third typhoid shot and am I glad, although they didn't hurt me.

We were really initiated the other day we had an air raid alarm (for practice) and you should have seen the people scurrying around. We have also gone through the gas chamber. We were given a lecture on how to put gas masks on and how they use them and about gases—mustard and Lewisite. Both of which were supposedly used in the last war except that the Lewisite was on its way across when the Armistice was signed and therefore it was not used. They also told us about Chlorine, Phosgene, and Clocopicin.

Then we were told to put on our mask and go through the gas chamber which has tear gas in it. Then if our masks weren't on tight, we would start crying but our class was 100% and no one had any trouble, but then he made us take off our masks and go through the tear gas. We learned that gas masks are useful.

The radio is really swell. We take sun baths in the afternoon, and I can carry it with me. It works swell on battery.

Our nurse who was in charge of our ward was detached and sent to Oakland. They took five from here, we are sent out by Washington, with very little notice sometime. Most of the girls are from around here. These girls went to Oakland where they are opening a hospital. The other two girls on the same floor as me are fighting over who is going to have charge. I think they have both been here about the same length of time.

I haven't been remembered by the government yet. We thought we got it in our last paycheck, but apparently, they send us a check from Washington.

This place is like every other nurse's home I've been in. One girl lost three pairs of nylon hose. Gee! I can't understand when we all make the same pay why they have to take things.

One of the boys said he would show me China Town (in San Francisco) this weekend, I think I'll take him up on it even if it is against the rules. They gave us the usual instructions that we were not supposed to go out with enlisted men or corpsmen, but I do so want to see China Town.

Tomorrow is inspection. I told you about or did I?—the captain lifting up the springs and finding some dirt. He restricted our boys for a week, but by persuasion they finally let them go out. Jeepers! Was he ever a grouchy old thing. They don't pay much attention to patients then.

I'm terribly sorry Bill McIntosh (Author's note: Esther's sister Lavonne's husband) had to go but we're going to have to forget ourselves for a while and get to work. We also had a lecture on that. Some of the girls here have gotten engaged or married a few weeks after being here. Our chief nurse tells us it isn't patriotic. That after spending all that money to get us here and for uniforms and what have you and then during times of war to quit is a disgrace to our profession. We are, to lay aside our lives and give them to the government. Nevertheless, a few are still getting married.

My warrant officer left on a furlough. Jeepers! People are here one day and gone tomorrow.

I must shine my shoes and fix my clothes and clean our room as tomorrow is inspection and I don't want my liberty taken away from me. Wilber (Esther's younger brother in the Army) thinks he will be going out soon. As we will probably be left here six months, we are now called "Boots" a very descriptive name, I think.

I will try to write a letter in Navy lingo sometime if I can.

Author's note: I don't know the gas she was referring to (Clocopicin), I couldn't find anything close to this spelling, all the rest of the gases she mentioned are lung irritants.

~

Thanks for the birthday greetings. One of our patients had a birthday today. He had some candy. We all ate. The Navy sent our sweaters and insignias. We have to start drill, Monday. Won't we be cute. We haven't our uniforms yet, but I suppose will soon have them.

I haven't met or seen anyone I know yet. There are quite a few people from Colorado but very few from Kansas.

We are having a lot of work now. There is a little difficulty on our floor due to two nurses. I hope they soon get their petty arguments over with so we can settle down to business. We managed to pass inspection this week by the chief. We certainly scrubbed to get it though. I'm still taking sun baths, but it was too cold today to take one.

I have really been seeing San Francisco. I got off at 1:00 pm Saturday and met a kid by the name of Showe at the bus station and he took me to San Francisco. We went to see "Mrs. Miniver" after which we ate spaghetti and meatballs. Then we took the oldest streetcar up a high hill and from there to China Town. China Town is an interesting place that is where we obtained those letters. The drug stores have herbs instead of drugs and the grocery store has pigtails and the inside of animals. He says that they eat them.

We went to a club called Lion's Den. It had Chinese waitresses and entertainers. They had the first Chinese Sally Rand (Author's note: Sally Rand was a famous fan dancer at the turn of the century). He also bought me a gardenia corsage.

We then went to a Mexican place where there were waitresses in Mexican costumes. They had Mexican dances. One was called a Mexican fun dance. A girl came out with high top shoes, unlaced a blackened tooth, and danced. Then she sat on a man's lap in the audience, and she kissed him. We went to the bus station from there, but the bus had already gone. So, I got a hotel room, and we went back the next day. I had to work at 2:00 p.m., but he bought my dinner before I went to the island.

Tuesday night we went back to San Francisco. As soon as we got there, we ate, then went to the international settlement where we saw many interracial couples. We went to a club which had an orchestra on one side, a bar, and the rest was filled with lounges. We stayed there for a while. He bought me a corsage with gardenias and roses.

Then in the international settlement we went to a place called the Hurricane. It was Hawaiian. The roof and chairs and tables with the sides were bamboo. In back of the orchestra was a sea rippling with a volcano and a ship. Picture somehow lights were fixed, so that the water seemed to ripple. All of a sudden, the lights went out and it sounded like hail on tin with lightning and thunder. We then went back to the Mexican place, and we left for Vallejo. It was really fun.

I haven't received the uniforms yet. Did I tell you that a shampoo and finger wave costs $1.25 out here? It seems they have a union.

Esther

P. S. He even paid for the Chinese letter, and he suggested it.

Author's note: Showe was my Mother's future husband and my father.

August 5, 1942

Excuse me while I dress for drill. They even have us marching— drilling wasn't half bad. We learned to salute the calls to keep in line. Friday we're to have inspection by the captain.

I am working in the afternoons now from 3 to 10. I'm the only nurse, we have about six corpsmen.

I celebrated my birthday in San Francisco. Showe took me to the theater, and we saw Al Pearce and his gang. It was really good. Then we had dinner.

He leaves this Saturday for Goat Island (Author's note: Goat Island is also known as Yerba Buena Island in San Francisco Bay. In WW II it was called the Treasure Island Naval Base and used as a location for transporting people and machines to the Pacific Theater.) I don't know when he goes from there. His ship is out. We did have a lot of fun. We also went to San Francisco Saturday and went to a show and visited several nightclubs.

We had our last tetanus shot today. I sure hope this one doesn't make me sick.

I just finished eating. We had fried chicken, mashed potatoes, peas, celery and onions, chicken gravy, and ice cream. It was really an excellent meal.

We received our sweaters which they issued us, and we bought our purses. It isn't worth the money that you spend, and they really could save money on the white uniforms. They practically drag the floor.

Excerpts from letters to her sister Alberta and her family

August 10-12, 1942

Did you ever get any more sugar? I still have my card, but I've never used it.

This institution is a rather large place and has a capacity of about 1,500 patients. Many of the older ones don't even know where all the buildings are. I work in a surgical ward. We have a lead capacity of 52. There is a large turnover practically every day. We keep them for about three weeks—appendectomies—and then send them to a convalescence ward. Where they remain until shipped out for duty. After they are up, they help with the work. The hernias remain longer. The patients do very well, considering everything.

The morning nurse works from 8 to 3. The afternoon nurse works from 3 to 10, and the night nurse covers several floors. The corpsmen do all the work, but it is really a job trying to find them and keep track of them.

I wish you a happy birthday, Bert. I had a lot of fun on mine.

Jean (a man's name). He's supposed to be German and Irish. He has real dark hair and eyes, took me to San Francisco; we went Saturday afternoon. We went to a show I practically get lost in the theaters. They are so large.

We ate and then went to a few nightclubs one was called the Chinese roof garden and we really had fun. They have lounges scattered about like in a large hotel and then a long bar with stools it is really interesting. The waitresses were boys and girls in Chinese costumes.

Excerpts from letters to her parents

August 14, 1942

Today was inspection. We passed OK and really the ward did look exceptionally nice.

I am awfully glad I brought my coat; we wear them every night. Tell Dad not to get in such a big hurry. We are still wearing civilian clothes and probably won't be in uniform for some time yet. (Author's note: Her father probably wanted a picture of her in uniform.)

Oh! You can also tell Dad the darn uniform overcoat and all is costing us $130. It had better be good. We don't pay for anything but our shirts, neckties, shoes, hose and gloves.

I'm going to San Francisco tomorrow to get a pair of black

shoes. We have to wear black Oxfords. I'm going to meet Jean there. Then we will probably go to the show. He asked me to marry him last time. Jeepers! I almost fell over but nevertheless he is a swell kid. He wanted to know what my folks would think, and I told him they would probably faint and be glad to get me off their hands. But don't worry I'm in the Navy now. We also do have a lot of fun.

We (my roommate and I) went to see a show last night at 11:00 PM. We didn't get out until 3:00 AM. They had two features and a Mickey Mouse. One sailor was lying in the aisle sound asleep. Some of these poor kids get back from battle first time they've seen shore in months and some two or three years, and they are worn out, but want to make a night of it. Having slept on decks, I guess a carpet would feel really good.

Did you ever find those pictures of us six kids? I can't remember where I put them and if you can find the one of me in that formal would you please send it? He wants a picture and that's the only one I have that you can't tell who I am.

Esther in her formal dress

September 4, 1942

We have gotten our shoes, hose and purses also our
shoulder boards for our winter coats. They are only a piece of
cardboard with gold braid on top, but they cost us 3 bucks. Two
of the girls are now in uniform. I have my Navy nurse's Insignia
for our duty uniform and our gold braid for our hat, so we are
on the last lap.

If you can't find those black hose, it is OK. I have several
pair here now. I got the last nylons that they had in Vallejo.

I've been working PM's this week and I have two wards, but
it really isn't so bad.

We went to San Francisco again last week. I met Jean there
and we went to another patient's house for dinner. It was delicious. We had spaghetti and meatballs with salad, green beans,
et cetera. It tasted so good. I stayed all night with them. Jean
had to go back at midnight. Her husband is in the Navy, and
she has a small child and is all by herself. We had a lovely time.

We went to the ball game next day. San Francisco played
Seattle. Seattle won. It was an open-air stadium, and I got a
lovely sunburn from it all. I'm peeling now. In the evening we
attended a newsreel. I really enjoy those. We didn't stay very
late because he had to go back again at midnight.

We had an interesting time about two weeks ago. We went
to a place called the Top of the Mark. It is a large hotel and at
the top is a lounge. In the center is a bar where drinks are
served, there are lounges and easy chairs all around. The place,
enclosed with glass, is 19 stories up and you can look out over
the city of San Francisco. It is really a beautiful sight.

We met a British sailor there. Their Navy doesn't have it
nearly as nice as we do. They aren't paid nearly as much as our
boys, and if they joined the Navy at the age of 14, they aren't
recognized until they're 16, and that two years just doesn't

count. He was really interesting, and his brogue was the most
peculiar. I love to listen to them talk.

I haven't called the lady yet, but Jean goes to duty Saturday
so I will have more time. They say we will soon have to wear
our raincoats and what have you.

September 13, 1942

We haven't been working very hard as our census has been
very low. We are expecting a convoy from the Solomons which
hasn't arrived yet.

I saw Jean again yesterday. He has left the hospital and is
stationed on Goat Island which is right off of Treasure Island.
He still wants me to marry him. He has more common sense
than a lot of people. He is 26 years old, a Catholic, but he
doesn't believe in the Catholic religion. He has been in the
Navy four years. His time was about up when the war broke
out. I think he's going to get the rings this week, but of course I
wouldn't marry him until after the war is over. He originally
came from Maryland.

I had better stop raving and tell you what goes on here. We
had a black out the other night. It seems that we aren't doing so
well at present. How is everyone? I've been putting in so much
time getting nothing accomplished. Our uniforms are due this
month, and I will have my picture taken as soon as we get them
all together. Gee! some of the kids had to get theirs altered and
it cost $12. I'm sending for my hats. They will cost $12.75.

Excerpts from letters to her sister Alberta Murphy and her family

September 23, 1942

I saw doctor Langhus, a doctor from home (a good one too). He's stationed at San Diego I talked to him for only a minute. He left his wife and child in Kansas City. He was an intern when I had charge of Bacdon (Author's note: probably the name of a medical ward in a hospital in Kansas City, Missouri).

We also received our dog tags today. Quite a few nurses from here are getting married.

Did you have enough sugar for canning or is it still as scarce as ever? We of course get all we want here.

I meant to tell you about our dog tags. The above diagram is the exact size in information T. Eight. 42 means our last tetanus shot. A is our blood type but the last time I was typed I was type (?) and one never changes blood type, but so much for that except that they have our fingerprint in the back. They are dipped into acid and there it remains until the metal wears away.

The picture I will have made as soon as I get my uniform. The folks asked me for one every time I get a letter and oh, how I hate to have it taken.

We also saw and heard Sophie Tucker sing to night some of the songs were ribald (don't look that one up) but how the boys enjoyed them. She also sang some old ones like "My Melancholy Baby" and "Shine on Harvest Moon." She's supposed to have introduced them. I wonder how old she is?

I have had a lot of fun up to the present day, but Jean was transferred to Boston. He came up last Thursday. He had to borrow someone's pass. I worked until 10:00 PM. He had to get the kid's pass back to him, so he left at 8:00 PM and I met him at Vallejo at 11:00 PM. We went to San Francisco, and he had to wire for some money for his ticket. The next day I had to be to work at 3:00 PM so I had to leave at 1:00. He wanted me to go to Maryland with him, but I still feel patriotic, so I didn't of course. He wanted me to marry him, but I was afraid I'd shock the folks.

I warned them though. If they don't take me seriously that's not my fault. Gee! But he'll probably go to sea right away and there I'll be though, and he's such a swell kid. So, I have to stay at home now. Although I was tempted with such an invitation as follows.

"You are cordially invited to attend a chicken dinner to be held anywhere you might name with an evening of very enjoyable entertainment. How about it? Chicken, watermelon, dancing, sparkling wine or conversation. Check your choice! Time is a wasting."

Why do people always try and tempt me with food? Am I a glutton? But I promised I wouldn't go out so here I am.

Oh! I must tell you about the party we had for our chief nurse (been in the Navy 20 years). She is leaving for Brooklyn and what a party. I believe the true name for it is a cocktail party with hors d'oeuvres, sandwiches (those you swallow in one bite). OK let's see. Strictly feminine all-in uniform. It's only the second time I've had liquor in uniform. I had to work so I only took one.

Excerpt from letters to her parents

October 28, 1942

Author's note: the stationary had a picture of Jesus and a Bible verse "Blessed are the pure in heart for they shall see God." Matt.5:8

Now for the story of this stationary. We had a brainstorm the other night and went to church. We were early, so they put us in the young people's division after which we went up to the evening meeting. We sang a lot of songs, and the preacher introduced several people. One was a chap going into the Navy.

Then he introduced a lady who has worked in jails, hospitals and houses of ill fame for 40 years or as she called them the cellar of the earth. She blamed everything on the church and home. She spoke frankly and firmly and, every once in a while, she went off into poetry. She was really a wonderful speaker. Her name was Colonel Herron. I'm enclosing a song she wrote. They gave us each a folder of stationery like I'm writing on. We had coffee and doughnuts afterwards at the nurse's home. We had a very enjoyable evening.

President Roosevelt cannot walk without assistance. I wasn't in that newsreel as I didn't go down, but I was there when Mrs. Roosevelt was visiting us.

I've had a busy day today. We got up at 7:00 AM, had breakfast, went to work at 8:00. Had our yellow fever shots at 10 AM. Then I made my stage debut at 12:00 PM. It was Navy Day, so four nurses (in uniform), four marines, two sailors and Mr. Wyner. I believe Mr Wyner is a former theatrical man. Jeepers! Can he sing.

We all sang "Buy Bonds." We sang the chorus, and he sang the verses, and he also wrote the music. It's never been played before. We might have launched a popular tune.

Buy Bonds

What Sherman said about war is right

How well we know it's true

and now that we are in this fight

here's what everyone should do

*Buy bonds, buy bonds to help our boys who are fighting over
    there*

Buy bonds, buy bonds and you will do your share

The axis started the war, but we've got to win

If you're not buying bonds now is the time to begin

Buy bonds, buy bonds and help to win this all-out war

The performance on Navy Day

It was really pretty—to evade all remarks about my singing voice, I was chosen for my legs. They also had a tap dancer and a sleight of hand artist. It was Navy Day, they auctioned off parts taken from the Japanese submarine. One bolt sold for $1,000 in war bonds. The man who went up didn't look like he had that much money.

The speaker was marvelous. He spoke straight from the shoulder. His name was Father Buins. He has been to Australia and what he didn't tell those workers wasn't worth telling. He told them that they were making more money than they had ever made in their lives. That they should be willing to give up their shirts for the boys who had given up families, homes, jobs, and everything to go and fight for their flag. While they stayed at their homes, firesides and with the ones they loved.

He said we would be ashamed of ourselves if we could see what those boys put up with. In heat of 110 degrees and 115 degrees all the time sleeping on the ground and at night. There were tears glistening in their eyes. He said that in the countries the Japanese had taken, these civilians had to be in at 6 PM to 6 AM, and not on the street. When they met a Japanese soldier, all of them, the civilians had to bow from the waist. Also, that when the Japanese took control, you didn't do the job you were best qualified for but the one they wanted you to do. In other words, he was disgusted at the attitude the people in this country were taking. He also said that Japan's army was a worse foe to us than Germany.

Excerpts from letters to her parents

November 6, 1942

The Russian has left. I think they must have gone back. He was certainly a nice person. We also have a man who came in with burns all over his face, but they have a new wax that they spray on now. It takes away a great deal of the pain, the muscles do not lose their tonicity, and the scar is not as prominent.

I go on night duty Monday night, and I am on for a month so if you don't hear from me, I'll be sleeping away. I work from 10:00 PM to 8:00 AM. It seems that those hours should be against the union. Are you going to have a Christmas dinner this year? I felt so sorry for the girls that went out. They don't know where they'll be.

We have a whole lot of new ones in now. We're supposed to have 150 but I think we're far over that now. This place and San Diego seem to be a distributing point.

We do our marching faithfully on Thursday and Tuesday. We are also doing exercise now. We should keep our figures trim.

Did I tell you I received three letters from Jean all at once? I haven't heard from Wilber for quite some time. They probably went across. Sometimes here they send a draft of corpsman out on 48-hour notice. So, you see they never know.

It takes so darn long to get off this island that unless you have a car you might just as well stay put at home. The buses were crowded before but now they'll be terrible with the gas shortage.

I guess I told you that Jean was a Catholic although he says he doesn't believe in it and is nothing.

November 12, 1942

The news the last few days has been so good. Six more girls have received orders, my roommate was one. They are going to Pearl Harbor.

Since I've been on night duty not much has happened. Our coats are in, so we won't have to freeze now. I received a letter from Jean several days ago. He wanted me to resign and marry him. If I put in my resignation, they wouldn't accept it unless I was already married.

We received a large bunch of patients. Out of 150, we got 10 in our division. We have a census of 81 but several eat at home, so we don't have them all. Many of them are up and about.

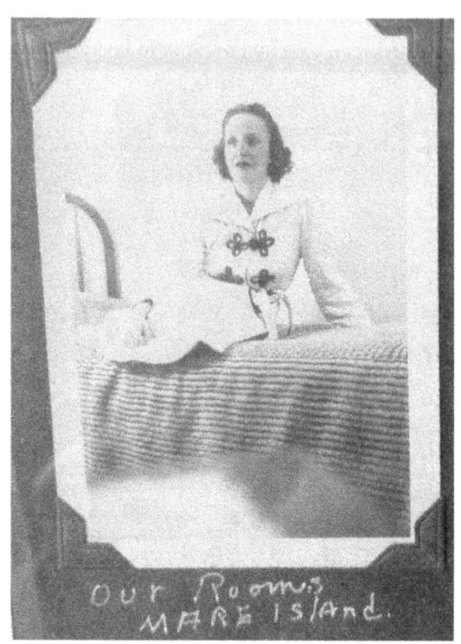

Mare Island in her room

November 14, 1942

Here I am again. We received another convoy of patients. 250 this time. All of the day girls were called back to duty. They let us night girls sleep. We work 10 hours a day. Anyway, we have boys in with shark bites and several other things, but most are psychoneurosis. They are really a wonderful bunch of patients, and some hadn't seen a bed for three months. Why, they were so appreciative of what we could do for them. It has been cloudy here. I guess the rainy season will soon be here.

Eight more people arrived today. Many of the corpsmen were killed during battle.

I heard from Jean this week. They were going to leave but where they were going, of course, is a military secret.

The day force cannot even go out over the weekend this week until we have all the patients straightened up.

November 26, 1942

Sorry I'm so slow, but these nights are really long sometimes. My roommate leaves for Pearl Harbor Thursday so I will probably get another one.

We saw and heard Kay Keyser last night. He was on the compound. I haven't heard from Wilber for a long time. Do you have any idea where he's at?

I heard from one of my former patients. He's back in doing swell. I must fix a box for Wilber, but I don't know what to put in it besides candy, toothpaste, razor blades, and a box of stationery and handkerchiefs.

I have only 12 more nights of night duty. We have to PH1/C (Author's note: this could be half pay or a pay cut) on now and it actually burns them up to think that they have to waste their time doing things like that. One can't blame them though. Some were earning as much as $300 a month, and they volunteered to come in. The civilians out here don't treat the boys very well. They really ought to put the civilian men on the same base as the enlisted men and let them earn only that much.

Excerpts from letters to her sister Alberta and her family

Late November 1942

I'll bet Bobby Bill has grown. Jean has a niece he had never seen until he was home. He said that she was spoiled.

I'm working nights now, so I don't get as much accomplished. My roommate is rather noisy, not talking but slamming drawers so I can't sleep clear through. But she's on PM's now so I come in and slam the doors and papers also the drawers so I'm just about even.

Night nurses, Mare Island

I heard from Jean about a week ago. They were leaving then. I don't know where.

We have had several groups of patients, one bunch had 150. The other 251. The girls on days have had to stand by and be ready to go but, being on nights I've never had to. One is all bitten by sharks. He looks awful, but they are really a cheerful bunch of boys.

Excerpts from letters to her parents

Author's note: This letter was probably written in December—the letter is a partial one, it's missing the first page, and there is reference to a picture she must have included.

Excuse the rambling. I'm still going to call up Bertha Schwab someday. I haven't heard from Verda for quite a while, but of course I owe her a letter. I also promised her a picture.

You may tell Virginia that we take only half of people to get more of California's beautiful scenery in and as you can see, we usually do.

My Aunt Anna and Uncle Ernest have really gone in for farming. I'm so glad though. Tell Mrs. Bloom (Author's note: her parent's neighbor after they moved into Clay Center from the farm) hello for me.

I bought a new pair of bedroom slippers in San Francisco yesterday. I bought a tie for Bill. It is a beautiful dubanay (that's not the right way to spell it, but it's a dark red) I hope he wants it. If not, write and tell me what he wants. All that I've heard is income tax lately.

I'm having the darndest time learning to tie that tie, so I got one that just snaps about the neck and all I have to do is hook it. Really wonderful when you're in a hurry.

I also got a box of cookies for Jean. I haven't the least idea what to get him for Christmas. Does anyone have any idea?

While walking down Market Street in San Francisco yesterday, a man walked up and asked me if I had a New Testament. He said he wanted all of the servicemen to have one and shoved it at me, so now I have a New Testament. From whom I don't know. I was in uniform. One lady walked up and congratulated me. What on, I don't know, but the average individual thinks that we are all Waves. So naturally we have a lovely time. I had lunch at a place called Holland Inn. The best chicken pie in the world, so the sign said, but I had a Roma red wine, rolls, butter, turkey and avocado casserole and a cup of coffee all for $0.75. I was still starved when I finished.

I had better stop this rambling. Tell Dad not to let the tire, sugar, and gas situation get on his nerves.

Gee! It's almost chow time and I must simply stop. I finished some Christmas cards, but I'm not giving much this year.

December 7, 1942

It was just a year ago today that we really entered. We haven't made so much progress yet.

The R. on N.N.C. means reserve or that I'm not a regular, only a reserve. We are working much harder now. I just finished my month of night duty (I'm writing this lying down so if you can't read it just stand on your head).

The Admiral was to make inspection today, but I don't know whether he arrived or not.

December 9, 1942

Sorry I was so slow in writing, but I've been so darn sleepy that I couldn't stay awake. I wrote one letter to Jean's mother and of course to Jean.

I want to tell you something, please do not think me bossy, but keep right on writing to Wilber just as you did before. He might not get them for a while, but many of the boys say that's about all they have, and it does their hearts good. One, as I've probably told you before, received his first last month since July, and was he ever thrilled.

The boys don't seem to mind fighting but there's one thing that seems to bother them, and that was that March on Washington by the last World War men and the reaction of civilians to them when they're out. The civilians seemed to think that it isn't their war. I've heard them gripe time after time about a few inconveniences on the buses.

We have been pretty fortunate to have a lot of food. Milk, meats, such as pork, etc. are hard to get out here for the civilian population.

Coffee is not served at a lot of places with meals. A good steak, if you can get it, costs $2.50 including the whole meal. Sugar isn't very hard to get, safety pins are practically unknown, and they think that a few things are hard to get along without. But another year and we're going without more.

Several girls received orders for Long Beach. They say that is good duty. It's near enough to Los Angeles and also San Diego that you can lounge on the beach. In other words, it's the playground of California.

I am up for my 6 month physical. Gee! It doesn't seem that I've been here for six months. I have one picture of Jean. It's not very good, but to ease your curiosity, I will send it to you in the next letter. I don't know whether I told you he has dark eyes and hair. He isn't handsome nor rich but he is a dear. His brother dabbles in politics. He is a Democrat.

How's the farm situation? Do they let you plant as much as you want to? Did you have to pay a duty on what you had in storage?

I must pay up my bills before I get orders. Our raincoats are in now. Lord, if we go to Long Beach, we have to wear white shoes and stockings.

From Esther's scrapbook, captioned, "Taddy" for Taddiken

December 15, 1942

It has been lovely here but today it is really cold. I was going to learn to play golf, but I guess will have to postpone it.

We went to the Officers Club last night, but it really wasn't very interesting. I can't seem to have much fun without Jean.

I haven't heard from Orin Bahr for quite some time. He was probably shipped out. They are here today and gone tomorrow. (Author's note: Bahr was a relative of Esther's in the Army.)

I'm working days now and we really have been working. I must write another letter to Wilber. Gee! It seems that I'm away behind. There is a bill in Congress for an increase in salary for us. I do hope we get it. We will be getting $150. That would really be wonderful. I still have my state dues. I guess I haven't received a statement yet.

We haven't had bacon here for a long time. Also ham, but that isn't so bad. I guess the civilians really have to go without.

How is the tire and gas situation? Do I draw for Aunt Ella's Christmas dinner, or do they draw names? We are going to draw names here and have a small Christmas tree.

December 21, 1942

I will have another picture taken in San Francisco. I will have to have one in civilian clothes for Jean because he isn't an officer.

I'm glad to hear the kids are all OK. Gee! It took a war to make Dad cut down on his gas. No wonder he's losing weight if he has to walk to the community sale or do they still have them?

We cut half of their landscaping in back of the hospital and made our own decorations. They were really clever. We cut some branches off a pine tree and used red holly berries. It was really attractive.

We haven't been working as hard lately. We had a young man of 27 die of pulmonary carcinoma.

Gee! Since Dad can't get gas, what does he do?

December 26, 1942

Here it is Christmas eve. It really is wonderful here. It has been raining for three days. We are going to San Francisco tonight for church.

Hope you have a lovely dinner. We had a lovely Christmas tree. They sprayed it with wax hung on lights and ornaments and then put on tinsel. It really looked like a frosted tree.

I received a year subscription to the Reader's Digest. It really was grand.

I haven't heard from Jean for some time. They are probably out and won't be back for several months.

Most of our patients left for the holidays. They all sent boxes of candy. It really tasted good. We drew names at the nurse's home. The rate was $0.50. I received two beautiful handkerchiefs with my initials on them.

I have a new roommate she is much better than the other. One of the girls just came in and asked if I wanted to go to the club. Some doctor needed an extra girl or three. We actually serve the same purpose as the USO girls do sometimes.

They had a free dinner and drinks at the club last night. We were of course invited, but I didn't go.

Excerpts from letter to her sister Alberta Murphy and family

December 30, 1942

It still seems like summer here. The hills around are now turning a lovely green after the rain. We were supposed to have had an earthquake here Tuesday morning, but of course I didn't feel anything. Although it was said that it knocked some lamps off of tables in San Francisco.

We really had a grand time although I wish I could have been there with you all. Write and tell me all about it, will you? I was so hoping that Jean would be here. I know curiosity is killing the folks, because now they ask for a picture of him in every letter.

We are really well fed here. We have meat twice a day, but no bacon. Coffee, we have plenty, also sugar, so we don't worry about that.

I had a day off yesterday and went shopping. I bought a foot-locker, and with my large suitcase, that should be enough. I will try to have my picture taken in the Navy nurse's uniform.

We had to have it (picture) taken again yesterday for our passes. I've had mine taken so often since I've been here, I'm getting used to it now. Gee! Was I fortunate I found three pairs of white silk hose yesterday? I thought that was very fortunate.

We received another draft. Almost all the beds are filled in our division now. These were mostly wounded men.

January 10, 1943

Secretary Knox is coming today for inspection so naturally we had field day again yesterday. I have laryngitis (I can't talk) now. Fortunate for those around me. I received two letters from

Jean and a cable from Wilber. I sent the cable home so that you all can read it.

Esther in 1943, California

I'm getting my raincoat this payday. I decided to get the $32.50 one because $50 is too much to pay. I received Jean's letters by V mail. I decided to write Wilber's and Jean's both that way. You can't get too much on them, but they travel faster.

We have our new passes to get in and out of the gate. We now have four passes, a dog tag around our necks, a yard pass, a pass good for any Navy Yard, and a button for our lapel with our picture. My picture was a little better this time.

I didn't smile in the picture because when I do my gold tooth shows. Jeepers! It's two o'clock. I must get ready to go to work.

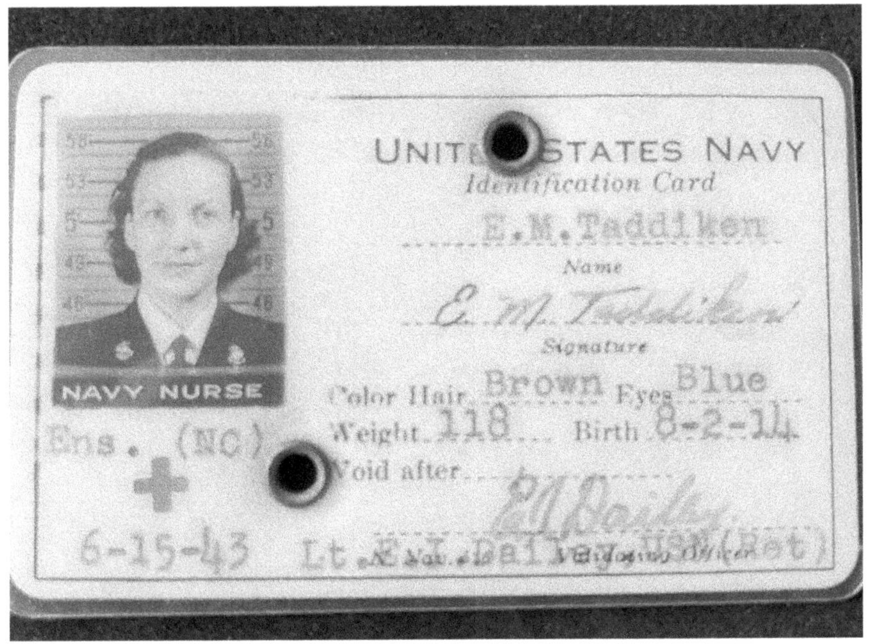

Excerpts from letters to her parents

January 21, 1943

We still need a bomb to make people realize a war is going on. Gee! It makes me so mad when I see how some of the people act. We are supposed to be polite, but sometimes we would sure like to haul off and hit somebody.

Several of the girls have gone to the opera. One night they were in the dressing room and a person all decked out in furs and jewels came in. She couldn't understand why they didn't keep the Navy out. I'm afraid I would have lost my temper and asked her what she was doing to help her country. People's true natures don't come out until they come against a difficult task and then it breaks through.

Would you send me Wilber's address again to make sure I'm putting the right one on?

We've been working rather hard lately, but we don't mind

that, I'm going swimming tomorrow. I haven't been for four days, and I do so want to learn to swim well.

Gee! It's almost chow time. I have so much to do, but the maid will vacuum the floor after chow, so I probably won't get anything done.

January 27, 1943

Things are much quieter here. I went to see the eye doctor this morning since I lost my glasses. My eyes have been all red again. I was doubtful for a few minutes whether I'd ever see again, because he certainly painted them up, but they feel better now.

I had another letter from Jean. I guess I told you about it. I'm trying to call San Francisco to get seats for the ballet. I've never seen a good one so if someone will change hours with me, it will be wonderful. We received another draft (of wounded men), so we'll be busy again.

January 30,1943

We had a lovely Christmas. Lawson and I went to church Christmas night at San Francisco. We had a lovely time. Sunday, five of we girls went to San Francisco to see "Blossom Time." It was really good. Mostly operatic numbers depicting the life of Franz Schubert. They were really beautiful numbers. We also went to the Grace Cathedral, which is really beautiful.

We have had several riots in Vallejo, between the white and black. It all supposedly began when a black cut up a Marine (no blacks in the Marines) with a knife. There were quite a few injured so now the boys on the island get no passes. I guess they are afraid of what will happen New Year's.

We did get our raise. It is going to be wonderful. We can at least buy bonds now. Some are afraid we aren't going to be able to cash them until ten years after the war, but I maintain if we don't win the war, they won't do any good anyway.

Have you heard from Wilber yet? I haven't heard for a long time. Neither have I heard from Jean. I wish they would hurry and get to port, but as long as I haven't heard of them being sunk, it isn't so bad.

January 30, 1943

I must dash this off rather hurriedly as it is almost time for chow. We go to work at 1:00 PM on Saturday which makes it a very long day. We were expecting a draft (of wounded men), but it hasn't arrived yet. They say about 800 this time so we will probably get them today.

I haven't heard from Wilber or Jean for some time, but I know they will write when they can.

We received our wage increase. I'm making some out for bonds. I still have to get a raincoat.

We are going to church tomorrow. We went last Sunday too. We went to the ballet Thursday night. It was the first I had ever seen. I enjoyed it very much especially the music.

February 8, 1943

We had a much quieter week. We attended a concert at Treasure Island. We hired a bus from the island, and about thirty of us went over. The San Francisco Symphony Orchestra played with Pierre Monteux conducting. Jose Iturbi played the piano. He played Rhapsody in Blue by Gershwin. It was lovely.

I hear over the radio tonight that the shoes are going to be rationed. I do hope they get it fixed so that everyone gets a fair deal.

I got another blue uniform and another white skirt. I still have to get a raincoat, another pair of black shoes, and a pair of rubber boots, and then I'll be ready to leave.

February 11, 1943

We have to march again. Captain's inspection. I guess he thought we should be snappy, and we didn't meet his expectations. We are also taking swimming lessons now. I have always had trouble breathing but I think I have it down now.

Gene Krupa was to be here tomorrow night, but it seems the government has served papers for illegal use of narcotics to minors, so I don't know for sure whether he'll make it or not.

I received another letter from Jean. He is having coconut milk, and he says there is nothing but native women. His address has been changed to San Francisco, so if they come in, they'll probably come in here. Gee! I hope so. I must stop raving and get to work.

February 14, 1943

A patient has been pestering me so much that I finally told him I would go out with him. We almost have our wardrobes complete. I'm going to get another suit, and I'll have to get a new pair of shoes. Hope they don't send me any place muddy.

Not much has happened, and I just finished writing to Jean. I received a letter from Jean's mother Tuesday.

$\sim$

February 18, 1943

We went to Holly's Monday. She has the sweetest baby. We had some lovely tea and cake. I'm going to take care of the baby some night. Tuesday night I went out with a patient. We went to San Francisco and saw "Random Harvest." It is a lovely picture. You should see it.

Wednesday another nurse and I went to San Francisco to get some shoes. I finally got a pair of black ones and then we went to the show. I must close now and write to Jean.

$\sim$

February 24, 1943

I received the enclosed letter from Wilber today and thought you might like to read it. It is beautiful here today. The sun is shining and no sign of rain.

Vern Reynold is going to be in San Francisco Saturday. I think Holladay, Oeceiall, Posen and I are all going in. We saw Dinah Shore last Sunday. She is really cute.

I haven't heard from Jean for quite a while. He was on the destroyer, the USS DeHaven, which was sunk at the same time the Chicago went down, so I probably won't hear for a while.

$\sim$

March 8, 1943

We had some more racial trouble last night between civilians and Marines involving liquor.

Last night, we went to a dance in San Francisco. We really had a good time. I finally paid my income taxes. Gosh! Were they ever high, but I don't mind.

I understand we pay as we go now, also that the farmers are not going to be drafted. It is really nice. They have cut us to coffee once a day at breakfast.

I had dinner with one of our patients Wednesday night. We had a lovely dinner and saw a show. I will tell Jean. It was so good to hear that he is alive.

We were going to have a citation for something or other. We had to get dressed twice. Once it rained and the second time the man had his cast off and couldn't walk. That was a little bit of all right about the Jap's ships sinking.

Do you think Mr. Bennett would have a small alarm clock, not electric? If so, would you get it, and have it sent out and then I'll pay you? It's impossible to get one here. It should be small, so it won't take up much room.

Excerpt from letter to her sister Alberta and family

March 9, 1943

I'm going to try and dash this off before we go swimming. It is really terrible when they give these girls advantages like that and so few take opportunity of it. It's all free. The only thing is that the pool is about two miles from the nurse's home.

I haven't heard from Jean since his parents were notified of his injury. I received a letter from his mother yesterday. She is rather upset.

We saw and heard the "Merry Macs" the other day. They came over and sang for us. Were they ever good.

We haven't been working as hard as usual because we haven't had a draft (wounded patients) in for quite some time and these are all patched up. All they can do is wait until orders come.

Excerpts from letters to her parents

March 19, 1943

It seems that Saint Patrick's Day is over, and Jean sent his love. I finally heard. He said that he was all right and not to worry. Gee! It was grand to hear from him.

Several girls received orders today, but all were to Idaho. Everyone has been asking me how it feels, but I didn't receive any.

A patient and I went to San Francisco to the Saint Francis hotel. We saw "In Which We Serve" first, then had dinner. All had music. There was a dance floor, an orchestra played during dinner. Palm trees were stuck at intervals around the place and there were large glass pillars between tables. He is supposed to be nuts, but if he is, so are we all. He went on a 90 day leave last night. I went with him to Crockett to catch the train. We were there on time, but they didn't announce them, so he missed it. He had a roomette on the first and had to take a Pullman lower on the next, which left at 9:30, and then I almost missed my bus. What a night.

We just came back from the Rodman. They had a stage show with singers, musicians and everything. It was free, so we didn't mind. We go down in buses, which cost us nothing. They usually are pretty good. We do work too.

It is beautiful here now. We walked to the yard post office

and all the flowers: tulips, pansies, spirea, etcetera. Gee! They were beautiful. On the way back, we met an officer's wife. She took us to their apartment. It was once the servant's quarters, and I wish you could have seen them. She has a small son that is darling. Her husband is a patient injured in action.

April 7, 1943

I haven't heard from Wilber for quite some time. I will try to go and see Jenny June, but Jean is coming back by here, and I don't want to miss him. Enclosed are some snaps we took. We were experimenting with those in uniform (white). We did it one day while we were on duty.

I told you about Lowry taking me out to dinner and to see Ted Lewis. He also brought me some beads, but he couldn't find me, so he took them home. He was married on his leave. He was a corpsman when I was on ward 18.

We have received so many patients in the last week that we've really been working. If we get another convoy in the next week, we'll have no place to put them.

Several girls have received orders in the states. Two went to Alaska. We have about twenty new ones that arrive this week.

April 17, 1943

Jean was supposed to arrive today but something must have happened. He sent me a telegram from Chicago, Illinois, but the train might have been delayed. I understand they're having floods.

Everything's fine here, except that I'm still working in

S.O.Q. (Sick Officer's Quarters) and we are working harder than we were. Jenny June sent a wire today saying she was going to Bakersfield. I called her but didn't go up as I was afraid Jean would come. Howard's wife answered. She seems very nice.

Sorry I neglected to tell you about Jean. His last name is Showe. He comes from Hagerstown, Maryland, is 26 years old, has brown eyes with black curly hair, rather dark. He has long eyelashes. He worked in Hagerstown before joining the Navy. He was brought up as a Catholic although he isn't a strict one. All I can say is he is a honey after most I've seen, and I've really seen a lot in my line of work.

I'm sending you his picture so that you can see what he looks like. I hope you like his looks. Gee! I sure hope you like Jean, and I think he's a honey. I must close now.

April 23, 1943

I wish you could see the country around here now, it is beautiful. I've never seen such large and lovely flowers. Roses all over. A small purple flower which seems to grow wild. They say it is a moss flower.

I sent the folks a picture of Jean. We didn't have enough for all, but you can see him then. He came back here from his leave. He is going to be a little late arriving at his station, but I hope they didn't punish him.

B. and I went to town last night. We were going to see Bill Robinson tap dance, but we met one of her former corpsmen, just back, so we had a few cocktails and then saw him off on a ten-day leave.

We went to the Golden State theater, but for the life of me, I can't remember the name of the show. They also had a stage show which wasn't anything exceptional.

Ever since I've been in the Navy, I've been roped in on committees. We are having a party, and I'm chairman of the invitation committee. We send blanket invitations, so it won't be so bad.

I'm going out with the mad Greek tomorrow night. He knows about my ring although we are not supposed to wear them on duty. I have a Donald Duck that a patient gave me so I'm sending it to Bobby Bill. You can tell him it's from a Marine.

It would certainly be swell to go fishing. We have to wear our uniforms most of the time so you can see what we would look like fishing.

April 25, 1943

Happy Easter! I received the box. Thanks a million. The cookies were delicious, but you shouldn't use so much of your sugar ration on me.

I also received a letter from Tiny, but haven't had time to answer it. Now that Jean's gone, I might get some work done. By the way, I sent you his picture. I hope you like him. I also sent Wilber a snap. Dad needn't bother about strangers; people are too easy to read. They're almost like a book.

Did you get the insurance straightened out? It kept me awake part of one night. And then I thought, Oh Hell! If they can go out and get shot up, I'm a fine one to worry about insurance. There's one thing our patients regret, and that is if they're fighting for all of these strikers that they ought to object. That is a court martial offense in the Army or Navy. Most think that shooting's too good for those people.

The Red Cross passed out Easter baskets. They were really beautiful to all of the patients.

Who got the alarm clocks? He wouldn't reserve one for me, would he, and call you as soon as they come in? My electric one won't run out in some of those places. And as there are 181 girls here now, and 20 more coming in with no empty bunks. Someone's going to take a trip.

May 1, 1943

I had two letters from Jean. He had a cold but he's OK now. He said that he might get a ten day leave and come down here to see me. I must shine my shoes now for inspection.

May 4, 1943

Jean is as swell as he looks. He is at Washington (state) now and is trying to get a twenty-day leave. I do so hope he gets it.

We went to see "The Keeper of the Flame" with Spencer Tracy and Katharine Hepburn. It really isn't very good.

Last night, the Mad Greek took me to Vallejo. We went to see a show and then we went to the Casa De Vallejo to have a cocktail. We had a nice time.

I've had a terrible time getting organized tonight, first the invitations had to be gotten out, and then the money for the party. We are giving a dance a week from Friday night.

I'm still working in S.O.Q. or Sick Officer's Quarters. I was hoping she would transfer me but no luck.

I must close now and write to Jean. I hope my junk isn't crowding you out. Thanks a lot, nevertheless.

<hr>

Excerpts from a letter to her sister and her family

Esther congratulated her sister on the birth of a daughter, Barbara.

May 20, 1943

It's grand here. The days are warm and the nights are cold.

We went to San Francisco to see "Life with Father." They were all redheads. Mother, father, and the four sons. We didn't stop laughing until it was over.

Did Bobby stay with Mother and how did they get along? Is he bashful? Gee! I'm going to have nieces, nephews, cousins, etc. that I've never seen.

I neglected to write to Wilber this week. I went to the park

with a former patient of mine. He was a Lieutenant Commander, but he had to walk all over the park with me. That's the
only way one can see anything. In one building they had cactus,
palms, and flowers of all kinds. Mostly foreign flowers and one
case had orchids white, lavender, etcetera. Were they ever beautiful. He cooked some ham, eggs, and chickpeas. Also some
Greek coffee for us. The chickpeas are what they make coffee
out of down South, or chicory, is also another name for it.

Two girls are leaving Saturday. They were married. One in
February, the other about a week ago.

Excerpts from letters to her parents

May 20, 1943

Our party is over so all I have to do now is work. We had a
good time at the party and a large crowd turned out. So, our
work wasn't in vain.

Several of us went to San Francisco to see "Life with
Father." It is a stage comedy and very good.

The nurses of the hospital were invited to a dance tonight. I
didn't go because I had some ironing to do. We frequently
receive invitations to various places. The Red Cross gave us
tickets to the circus. I had made a previous appointment at San
Francisco.

We had to drill this afternoon. I think they are going to take
some pictures and then discontinue it until next fall.

We went to the Golden State Park last Sunday. It was a
beautiful day. I wish you could have seen the house with all the
flowers. It was lovely. They had many foreign specimens. Then
we got halfway around on the fish, and it was closing time.

You don't still have that horrible picture in Penney's window,
do you?

May 31, 1943

It is lovely here. Such a nice sunny day. Guess who was here yesterday? None other than Rudy Vallee in person. Constance Moore and several others were also here, including Barbara Stanwyck.

Several girls received orders, but they were all for the states, which makes it wonderful. I have had a cold for the last week, but it is all cured now. Haven't heard from Jean for quite some time, but I did get a lovely box from him.

I have been bounced around like a rubber ball the last week. I would work one day in the office and the next day in SOQ, and this week I've worked in the chief nurse's office. Therefore, the typewriter which I'm trying to master, and I'm really proud of my accomplishment so far.

We have a very good galley. (Author's note: a galley is Navy speak for a kitchen or in this case a cook). He feeds us almost every night since we've been here. One night, we had coffee and snails, and the next night, we had coffee and apple pie which really isn't bad.

The other girl that is on with me is at chow now. So, it is nice and peaceful here. We went into Vallejo to see "This is the Army." It was really a good show and well worth your time seeing if you get a chance.

I had a lovely card from Jean's mother. I'll have to write to her tonight. I had to get up for Captain's inspection this morning, so I didn't really get much done in the line of work.

June 6, 1943

Time certainly flies here. Just think on the 29th, I will have been here a year. It really doesn't seem possible. I'll be glad to go in with the kids, and I'll send the dollar to Arlene. Excuse me, it'll be a dollar and $0.50.

Will you write and give me the exact date of Barbara Ann's birthday so I can put it in my book? I'm glad you copied the letters from Wilber. I haven't heard in quite a while. I write to several of the boys that I worked with, and I haven't heard from them for some time.

How's the wheat and everything at the farm? We have a corpsman from Arkansas. They have about 400 acres. His foster father is about 57 and unable to do the work. His mother can't do it either, and they have an adopted daughter of 12. The Farm Bureau has written and asked that he be deferred. He was doing all the work before he came in. I surely hope he makes it. He told us we'd all be welcome to come and get some fried chicken —gosh! It sounds good. We've had mostly ham.

If you have time, you can get the book from the library called, "I Served on Bataan" by Lieutenant Redmond. I'll bet the kids are getting cute.

I'm sending you an anchor. We wear them on the lapels of our ward uniforms and also our street uniforms. It will come in a separate box.

I received two letters from Jean the other day. He sends his love. I packed the other pictures and sent them to his mother. She said they really looked real. She has asthma quite badly. By the way how's Mrs. Paro? Hope she's OK.

My week of call is almost up. We have a week of call called the Disaster Unit. My week was this last.

Tomorrow I'm going to Vallejo and will send you a money order of $112. I also need a checkbook. Would you have the

hank send me one and also my statement of how much I've got?
I really must close now and get to work mending clothes.

Write when you have time—but please don't say anything
about fried chicken.

Excerpts from letter to her sister Alberta Murphy and family

June 7, 1943

The folks copied Wilber's letters. I haven't heard from him
for quite some time. I try to write once a week. When you're
feeling better and have time, get the book "I served on Bataan"
by Lieutenant Redmond. Gosh! It's gruesome. I've stopped
worrying though. Hard work always takes its place.

I hear from Jean about every other day. I do hope I get to see
him again before he leaves. He's not as handsome as he is a
grand guy. I could rave on for hours, but it would probably be
boring to you. I have some pictures of his family here. I guess I
told you they live in Maryland.

I got me a G.I. regulation raincoat. I'm getting so tired of
uniforms, I could shriek. I'd even help Bill put up hay in a pair
of overalls.

I'm celebrating my year in the Navy the 29th of June. I guess
I'm getting old to be in it. I surely don't feel it. Anyway, I've met
some swell people and had some interesting experiences.

I've been working mornings all week now. I've actually been
promoted. I'm in charge of SOQ now. It's more like a hotel. Do
you know of anyone who has a hotel? I can actually do everything but the menu now. We usually only take officers in
(Marines and Navy), but now we have a Colonel in the Army
and a woman patient in the Marines, and to think I joined the
Navy to get away from women—Oh well!

Please whatever else you do, don't mention fried chicken. We eat ham, but I don't mind. In that book (Back to Bataan), they ate horse meat and a monkey. They ran out of food.

I have to stay in this week. They said in the paper that Japan is going to bomb us July the 4th so, they have organized a Disaster Unit, where we aren't allowed to go out unless someone else takes your call. So here I am.

Sally Scyler Brown was up here last night with Oeceall. They are both from Research (Author's note: Research is the hospital where Esther took her nurse's training). Sally got a divorce and is joining the Army Air Evacuation Corps. Isn't it wonderful?

Excerpts from letters to her parents

June 8, 1943

We went down to see a Victory Review tonight. It was really good. and last night we saw "Reap the Wild Wind." It was beautiful. I had seen it once before.

I haven't heard from Jean for about four days so, apparently, they sailed. How many bonds do I have? They're making a survey, and I'll be darned if I know.

June 19, 1943

About twenty more girls are leaving, and I'm still here, but I guess I shouldn't complain.

We've had several days of really hot weather and then it cools off so much that you have to wear a coat.

I'm still working in SOQ. By the way, how many bonds do I have now? I received the checkbook and the sunsuit OK. Thanks a lot.

Some of the girls are going to the South Seas. Others are stationed in the US. Some of them here a very short time. There are three of us left here now.

We haven't very many patients at the moment, which makes me very happy because the fewer we have, the fewer injured.

I haven't heard from Jean for several days, but when they're out, one doesn't expect to hear very often. We've been going to Vallejo to see the shows. We saw "Oxbow Incident." "Life begins at 8:30," and "The Human Comedy." "The Human Comedy" was very good.

We had a Marine, part of the women's reserve. They finally took her away. She was a mental case.

One of the patients brought us a watermelon. Was it ever good. The corpsmen and we nurses ate it. We eat practically all the time. How are you coming with your ration coupons? I'm going to use my other shoe ration ticket pretty soon. I told you I've gotten your raincoat.

June 24, 1943

I received your letter day before yesterday, and was I ever glad that you'd heard from Wilber. I hope he's still OK. I received a letter from Jean. They're at San Diego now. I don't know how long he'll be there.

We went in to see the "Ice Follies." They were really wonderful. They had many costumes while they skated and danced. Last night Ostgard and I went to see "The Firefly." She is leaving for a ten day leave at Los Angeles. Tonight, we went to see "The More the Merrier." It is really a cute show.

About twenty girls have gotten orders lately but me it seems. Will you send me that pair of brown slacks? It seems that bugs are more prevalent in the South Seas. So, I'll use the slacks to protect my legs.

July 6, 1943

I came home, took one look at the work I had to do, and decided to write letters. Anything for an excuse not to do it. Ironing, washing, shining shoes, etc. My roommate is on a ten day leave so she'll probably be back next week.

I'm enclosing a letter from Wilber. I received it today. I sent him a birthday card. Hope he gets it. I am also enclosing a write up about two Navy nurses. Hope you enjoy it.

I received the slacks today. Thanks so much. Wasn't there a brown blouse? I finally bought a red jacket. Could you find out the names of some large department stores in Topeka or Manhattan and see if they have any black nylon hose size 8 ½? Just send me the names, and I'll write to have them sent COD (Authors note: cash on delivery). Mine are wearing out. I've been in the Navy too long.

I just finished cleaning up the baggage room. I don't think it's been cleaned since the last war.

I had a telegram from Jean last Wednesday. He wanted me to meet him in San Francisco, but I was already there, so of course I didn't get it until about 2400. I tried to call, but he wasn't there.

Oh, yes! I just finished having my eyes examined. My vision is OK. Those other glasses were nothing but glass. I'm exercising them now and they're much better.

July 15, 1943

The letter head on this stationary is from the Pepsi-Cola Center for Servicemen, Liberty Building, Market and Mason Streets, San Francisco, CA. We're waiting on the bus, so I'll dash off a few lines. They have a lovely lounge here for the women personnel of the forces. You can fix your nails, take a shower, write letters, telephone, play a piano, play the phonograph, play ping pong, and have a few Pepsi colas, etc. It is cleverly fixed up in greens, red, blue, tans, etc.

I haven't heard from Wilber lately. You have the last letter that I received from him. I also received the slacks OK. Thanks a million. I'm enclosing $50 from my paycheck. I think I'll go down to San Diego and see Priscilla, George, etcetera, and also, Jenny June. I haven't had my ten days leave yet. I could fly home, but I decided that would take longer.

I finally found three pairs of black rayon hose. It is really wonderful. They aren't so handsome, but they'll wear.

I just finished one of the best colds one could hope to have. I spent three days in bed only. It started only after I started taking vitamins for my eyes.

Lowry and his brother were here. We went out for dinner and dancing, and did we ever have fun. It was more fun than a picnic.

We went to some friends of Scotty's for dinner, or rather, we prepared the dinner. It was good. We ate our hearts because they don't take up as many points.

Could you find an alarm clock in Idana, Morganville, or some of those small places?

A snapshot of friends from Esther's scrapbook

July 19, 1943

I'm dashing this off before I have to go to work. I'd love to come for Tiny's (Author's note: her sister Lavonne) wedding, but I don't see how I can.

A letter from her brother John Wilber Taddiken stationed in Sicily, Italy

August 11, 1943

Dear Et,

Thanks for remembering my birthday with the card. It was really cute.

Those fellows were right when they say there is no glamour in war. At least not where the fighting is going on, but of course somebody has to do it. This looks to be a colorful island in peace time. These Sicilians have two wheeled carts which are a sight to see. On the sides are bright paintings of ancient Romans. The tailgate and axles are carved with figures of the saints all painted in bright colors. The mules or horses are decked out in bright red harness with plumes on their heads.

One fellow who was here before the war said that the harbor was filled with sailboats with patched sails of different colors, and it was really beautiful. Of course, they aren't there now.

Write often,

Wilber

~

Excerpts from letters to her parents after she had been home on leave

August 15, 1943

Yes, I arrived OK. It was a very eventful trip. The train was about 1/2 hour late. A WAC got on. She was going to San Francisco, so we made the trip together. We had to stand up until we were almost to Denver. People were sleeping in the aisle and the baggage racks. When we got to Denver, we just changed cars. We were fortunate in that it was air conditioned. The meal service was almost impossible. They sold box luncheons on the train. We usually got a hot breakfast. There was a family in the two seats in front of us. When we walked through the other coaches, they were really old fashioned. I thought those had all been junked. Every time we stopped at a station, everyone would dash to the nearest place that had food—it was really funny after a while.

The conductors called out no station except Reno. We stopped at quite a few to pick up mail. There was no water in the heads to wash your hands or face. Even the toilet couldn't be flushed, and there were a lot of children on the train. At every station, a group of women with brooms would come on board and sweep up, and the junk they got off was terrible.

They would collect our tickets, give us a stub, and before we reached that conductor destination, they would collect our stubs and give us back our tickets. I've never had such an experience.

I got back Sunday morning. We were on time. Must be because we subtracted so much time. I can think of no other reason.

I slept on the bus from Oakland to Vallejo. It was the shortest trip on the bus I've ever made.

Author's note: Esther must have received orders that she was being sent overseas.

August 30, 1943

There really isn't much you can send me except a waterproof secondhand watch, a cheap one, because they say they rust out there. Otherwise I have everything.

We probably will be gone for about 18 months. They will not take us nearer than 1,000 miles of the battlefront so there's nothing to it.

Jean's address is: Mr. Jean W Showe, WT 1/c, USS Harding, New York, New York, % Fleet Postmaster

He changes so often that it's hard to keep track of him. He was in New York the last I heard.

You should see our wardrobe. It's mostly cotton and uniforms. I'm not buying any new clothes except what's worn.

My roommate also received orders to the USS Solace. It's a hospital ship, but it goes into port frequently.

I must close. We worked from 0800 to 2100 today, and I'm so tired. We got around 300 boys tonight and were they ever glad to get back. They're such cute kids. The one I admitted tonight was only 18. I could hardly believe it and people blame them for getting drunk.

September 9, 1943

I haven't heard from Jean for almost three weeks now, but they have probably gone out. I'm still catching up on my debts, so I'll send some money this payday, and I found some lovely wool blankets. I think I'll send one home if you don't mind.

I went to the club the other night to dance. We went to the show first. You should see, "So Proudly We Hail." It's about the nurses on Bataan. Isn't it wonderful about the surrender of Italy?

One of the newspaper clippings that Esther kept

September 14, 1943

It's been grand here, nice and cool. We have started drill
again two hours a week. We have a Lieutenant in the Marine
Corps to drill us. He is a patient at the present time and is
awaiting orders. I received your letter and all the clippings.
They were really interesting.

I fixed Wilber up a box and am mailing it as soon as I get
some heavy paper to wrap it. I still have a month to fix Jean's.

I haven't heard from Jean for almost a month. But when they
go out, they go for business. As a result, they seldom come near
a mailbox.

Do you ever listen to Walter Winchell? He comes on Sunday
night and is very educational. He's the only one I know that
doesn't go miles to get an inch. Otherwise, he's concise and to
the point.

Two more girls received orders to Olathe, KS. They are
detached tomorrow. Many of the people I worked with when I
first came out are back as patients.

September 24, 1943

I really enjoyed Wilber's letter. He certainly does write interesting ones. You were probably wondering why I haven't written. It seems the government has found my name, so I'm
headed for the South Pacific about November 1st. I'll tell you
several things I would like to have you do.

#1. About Christmas, renew my subscription to the Reader's
Digest.

#2. I have marked two patterns of silver. I want sterling if
Bennetts or Buckners carry one of these or one similar, will you
order it and pay for it out of the allotment, which I will have

made out? I would like a full setting for six and the table-
spoons, etc.

#3. But before you get the silver, get a wool blanket (blue).
Oh, that is about all, be sure it is marked all wool.

#4. At the first of the year, please pay my life insurance. I'll
take care of my alumnae dues. That is about all.

Oh, yes! I'm sending Mrs. Showe your address. Hers is 228
South Mulberry St., Hagerstown, MD. I haven't heard from Jean
for quite some time, but I think I will soon.

I must close now. Don't you worry. I'll be okay.

September 25, 1943

I sent an air mail yesterday, but I forgot to ask you to put in
those green slacks and two pairs of white gloves. Do you think
you can get them here before November 1st? I'd surely appreciate it.

I've been so busy getting my supplies ready. We take enough
to last for two years. I'd really appreciate it if you take care of
the silver for me. I'll probably have to write several checks, so
will you watch the account, and if it gets too low apply the
allotment to my checking instead of banking? But I want to
make all the interest I can.

**Excerpts from letters to her sister Alberta Murphy and
family**

September 26, 1943

I'm dashing this off rather fast. Do you think it would be
possible to have your phonograph fixed and sent to me? I have

received orders to leave November 1. Will probably be in Frisco
for a while.

Excerpts from letters to her parents

October 11, 1943

I received the package OK and thanks a lot. Now will you
send me my raincoat? It seems they want $17.50 for them out
here and I'm Scotch.

I received a letter from Jean yesterday. He wants me to
marry him instead of going. He's been out there. I don't know
how I can get out of it now even if I wanted to. I'm practically
all packed. I made my allotment out for $120.

It's my December's pay. You will get it about January 5th.
Keep about $300 in my checking account. Put the rest in bonds.
Deduct my expenses and take any if you need it.

I wrote two checks for $40 and $50, so that leaves about
$200 on my checking account. I will probably send you some
more before I leave. We will be in Frisco for a while, but they
pay us for it. However, they have a very complicated system, so
we don't know when we'll be paid.

My roommate received orders to the USS Solace. Keep
writing to the same address as they forward our mail.

Excerpts from letters to her sister Alberta Murphy and family

October 17, 1943

This is much simpler. Thanks for getting the phonograph
ready, but I just barely got my radio in my trunk. This is one of

the worst jobs I've ever undertaken. To pack 18 months would even stump the king, but we're making it.

My roommate leaves tomorrow. She is going on a hospital ship which is really supposed to be good duty. Thanks for your wishes. I'll be OK as the years of perseverance I have had haven't been in vain. Just be sure and write. Thanks for the pictures of the kids. I have quite a collection now. I sent some on to Jean, so he won't feel as if he didn't know any of the family. He is really a honey. I'm so glad he's in the states now.

Helmstein just came back from the club. "Bebe" has a birthday tomorrow, and so they went to the club for dinner. Who said business was dull?

I have the duty "house mother." They've changed me around so much that I wonder if I'm versatile or just no good. I have a $25 bet on that I won't make "19" (Author's note: probably a rating in the Navy). You can actually have more fun as an ensign.

Jean has gone up two rates since I've known him. I really think it's wonderful. Gee! I wish you all knew him. His mother has sent me several pictures of the family. She must be adorable.

We are having a dickens of a time packing now. I really must fill the Coke machine and get ready to close up the place.

October 17, 1943

If you can't get the watch just don't bother. I thought maybe you could get one of those dollar watches that men have. They say they rust over there.

We are all packed to go. There isn't much we can take. I told you about the allotment; we get 10% on our wages which starts as soon as we're detached. Gee! I hope I don't get seasick. It's rather chilly here tonight.

I'm writing this on duty. I'm what is known as the house mother, a very thankless task. We count the linen, answer the phone, see that the girls are called when their boyfriends arrive, and put on the lights which is really a task. Also, empty and fill the Coke machine.

Tony leaves tomorrow. She is going to a hospital ship which makes the second roommate I've lost.

Jean is still in the States. I'm so glad for his sake. He has had enough of the battles to last for a while. I do hope you write to Jean. He would love to get a letter from you. Please don't worry about me because I will be all right.

I went to Frances' yesterday. She has some pinking shears, so I used them to cut off the tail of some of Tony's and my shirts. Business is slow right now—another hour and 1/2 and I can go off duty. You can go right around the corner and our room is there.

I really think $70 is too much to put into a watch. Did you send my raincoat? Have you heard from Wilber lately? I'm getting a pass to mail my box tomorrow. I will send it railroad express. Take good care of Jean's letters.

According to Esther, she left the continental United States on October 25th, 1943. Her orders state she was re-assigned to U.S. Naval Mobile Hospital No. 6 on November 30th, 1943 in Wellington, New Zealand, under the command of the U.S. Pacific Fleet, South Pacific Fleet, South Pacific Force Service Squadron.

NAVY SERVICE IN THE PACIFIC, WWII

Esther traveled to Noumea, New Caledonia on the USS Rochambeau (AP-63). According to "Wikipedia, Transports of the United States Navy," the Rochambeau had been a French ship in the Philippines taken over by a crew of downed US Navy fliers from Patrol Wing 10 and French sailors not supportive of the

Vichy government, established in France by Germany after the fall of France in 1940. They sailed the shanghaied ship to San Francisco.

The Marechal Joffre, as she was then known, was transferred to the U.S. Navy and commissioned on April 27th, 1942. She was renamed Rochambeau and converted for use as a casualty evacuation ship. On her first assignment for the U.S. Navy, she departed Oakland, California on October 20th, 1942, carrying replacements and reinforcements for the Guadalcanal campaign. She disembarked her passengers in Noumea, and replaced them with casualties from there, at Suva, and at Bora Bora before returning to San Francisco. The Rochambeau continued voyages to the South Pacific in 1944, exchanging passengers for casualties. Her last run was from November 16th, 1944, to January 17th, 1945.

Probably the Rochambeau's most famous passenger during her South Pacific runs, was Lieutenant (jg) John F. Kennedy when she carried him to Espiritu Santo where he transferred to LST-449 on his trip to the Solomons.

Esther was headed to a system of U.S. Naval Hospitals set up in the South Pacific to take care of casualties from battles to push the Japanese out of the southern South Pacific. The one exception to the U.S. built mobile hospitals where she served, was her duty station in New Zealand, where the government of New Zealand turned over a newly built hospital to the United States. If you are interested in the Naval mobile hospitals, vintage film exists of the Seabees building a Navy mobile hospital on Espiritu Santo, New Hebrides. It is Internet Archive, Naval Photographic Center Film #759. National Archives Identifier: 75661.

BACKGROUND ON U.S. NAVAL MOBILE HOSPITALS

The background information on U.S. Naval mobile hospitals was found in <u>History of the Medical Department of the U.S. Navy in WWII</u> [Chapter 1]. In 1939, when world war appeared imminent, the Bureau of Medicine and Surgery realized the need for some type of prefabricated hospital that would be completely self-sustaining and transportable. It also needed to be set-up without skilled craftsmen.

The mobile hospital was a 500-bed, completely equipped, transportable type, general hospital with self-contained power, water, commissary, laundry, and repair facilities. U.S. Naval Mobile Hospital No. 1 was first set up at Guantanamo Bay, Cuba, in November 1940, where it served local and fleet units. Mobile Hospital No. 1 paved the way for better mobile and base hospital construction.

Later mobile hospitals contained the following facilities: (a) water purification and softening plant; (b) storage spaces for supplies; (c) laundry; (d) galley; (e) automotive and ambulance equipment; (f) fire-fighting equipment; (g) light and power supplies; (h) refrigeration facilities; and, x-ray, dental, laboratory, and other equipment and facilities of a general hospital.

BACKGROUND ON NEW CALEDONIA

New Caledonia is a French collection of islands in the southwestern Pacific Ocean, about 900 miles east of Australia. It includes the island of New Caledonia (Grande Terre [Mainland]) where the capital, Noumea is located; the Belep Islands; and the Ile des Pins. New Caledonia also includes several far-flung uninhabited islets.

According to Wikipedia, in September 1940, New Caledonia joined the Free France organization, founded June 1940, after the June

1940 Fall of France. In March 1942, an agreement was made between Free France and the United States for a base in New Caledonia. In July and August 1942, Seabees arrived and began building the Naval Base.

Naval Base Noumea was a major United States Navy sea and air base at Nouméa, New Caledonia. Naval Base Noumea was built at Noumea Harbor. Noumea was picked for a Naval Base as it was beyond the range of Japanese land-based planes. Noumea is on the east side of the Coral Sea, 913 miles from Brisbane, Australia.

The Base was built during World War II to support the many ships and aircraft fighting and patrolling in the South West Pacific theatre of war. Naval Base Noumea had anchorage for large ships. Noumea was protected against submarine attack by a ring of islands and Naval minefields.

At its peak, 50,000 Troops were stationed at Naval Base Noumea. New Caledonia has been a colony of France since 1853. Noumea is the capital City of New Caledonia on the southwest end of the island. On November 8, 1942, US Navy South Pacific headquarters moved to Noumea.[1][2]

Esther probably worked briefly at U.S. Navy Mobile Hospital No. 5 in Noumea after her trip to the South Pacific on the USS Rochambeau in November of 1943 before she moved on to the U.S. Navy Mobile Hospital No. 6 in Wellington, New Zealand in December of 1943.

Although there was another hospital in Noumea, U.S. Mobile Hospital No.7, I believe Esther was stationed at No. 5 based on drawings from menus and memos in her scrapbook that resemble the drawings in the yearbook from US Fleet Hospital 105, also known as Navy Mobile Hospital No. 5.

In August of 1943 the designation Mobile Hospital was changed to Fleet Hospital. New serial numbers were assigned by adding 100 to the old number, except for Mobile Hospitals 1 and 2, which became Fleet Hospitals 1 and 2 respectively.

U.S. NAVY MOBILE HOSPITAL NO. 5, NOUMEA, NEW CALEDONIA ALSO KNOWN AS US FLEET HOSPITAL 105

My information on U.S. Mobile Hospital No. 5 comes from a donated yearbook from December 25th, 1944 that appears in an online medical unit database for Fleet Hospital 105.

In the yearbook, according to T.C. Ryan, Lt. Commander (MC) U.S.A. Historian, the hospital was formally commissioned on November 23rd, 1942, four days after the first patients arrived from Guadalcanal. Through the remainder of 1942 and through 1943, hospital and medical care was provided to patients from Guadalcanal, Tulagi, Bougainville, New Georgia, Treasury, Makin Islands, Della La Della, and other land actions as well as from the fleet.

During the year 1944, the hospital was improved continuously for the comfort and welfare of patients and staff. Patients were received from action in and around the Marianas Islands and other areas of the South Pacific.

Esther brought back objects her patients made in a hobby shop in a Quonset hut on base. They might have been made in Noumea or more likely at her duty station in the New Hebrides. They include a ship in a bottle, a salt and pepper shaker set made of artillery shells in a wooden stand, and a letter opener with the name Solomons carved in the handle. They also crafted her a small wooden trunk.

V-mail letter from Esther's brother John Wilber Taddiken, who was in the Army in Sicily

October 24, 1943

Well, I hear you finally got what you've been wanting. If it's anything like the Army, I know it's hell. Here's wishing you the very best of luck, and I usually do think it's grand of you nurses to go overseas.

I received your September 8th and 22nd letters last week but have been pretty busy in the daytimes, and we ran out of candles so I couldn't write at night.

If you're on New Guinea, you might run into Ed Fox or Elmo. His girl wrote that she thinks he is there too. I don't know why but I never seem to run into anyone I know, and there are quite a few here from around home. Got a letter from Tiny. They had just moved into an apartment in Austin. Hope you're getting along OK.

Love,
Wilber

~

Esther's letters to her parents

November 17, 1943

How's everything in Kansas? I'm sorry I didn't write before but there just wasn't anything to write about. I'm alright so you won't have to worry about me, although you might have to send me some clothes later on. I'm not just sure of what I'll need now.

You received my letter with my new address I hope. If not, you can get it off this one. I wrote one to Wilber today. He should be about due for a vacation, shouldn't he?

We saw a show the night before last, it was really cute. It was a Navy picture but all about shore leave so it was interesting. I haven't heard from Jean for quite a while. It will probably take longer for his letters to get here.

We made a trip to ship service, but I forgot my airmail stamps. I go to work tonight. It will seem funny to wear a ward uniform again. It seems so long since I've had one on. I didn't receive the watch but mine is doing pretty good, so I won't have to worry about it.

It seems that I spend my time washing and ironing and then I'm never get through. We seem to always be dirty. I just hope someday I'll get them all cleaned up. Almost time for chow so I'll have to get ready for it.

We heard "Henry Aldridge" last night. I just love to hear him. Maybe I'll get to go swimming tomorrow.

A postcard showing The Cathedral, Noumea, New Caledonia,
November 1943

November 25, 1943

I received a letter from you today dated November the 12th. It was really grand to hear from you. I also enjoyed Wilber's letter which you had added to your own.

What happened to Barbara's ear? You said that it was getting along fine now. Gee! How I would love to see the kids. They must be awful cute. How does John Vern like school by now? I was going to try and get them some postcards but as yet haven't gotten them any. I also tried to get a salt and pepper shaker for Nonie's collection but I'm having an awful time finding them.

Tell Mrs. Bloom and Johnson and everyone else hello. Has Verda been up lately? Oh! Yes, Uncle Phil and Aunt Susie sent me some evening in Paris perfume, so I wrote and thanked her for it. I have been doing everything in such a hurry that I don't do such a good job.

There are a lot of people we know here so it isn't so bad, and what a lovely Thanksgiving meal we had today even cranberry sauce. I might have to have some things later on, but if I do, I'll let you know. The watch hasn't arrived yet, but I'll let you know as soon as it does.

I haven't heard from Jean lately, but it will take much longer for his letters to get here.

The water is grand here but not quite as clear as Wilber said that it was. They say it is clearer in some places. I definitely don't like the taste of it, and it ruins one's hair, in fact mine is changing color again.

I thought I might see "Red" but, as yet, I haven't come in contact with him. (I think she means Red Young, a relative).

Did you get my scrapbook and books all right? One of the girls said that she would send them for me as I didn't have time.

December 12, 1943

I received your letter written on October 25th and, also the V-mail letter on the same day. Needless to say, I was glad to hear from you and that everyone is all right.

I haven't received the watch yet, but it should be here any day now. I sent a cablegram which I hope you received. It is really grand here and our quarters are delightful.

Have you heard from Jean? I haven't heard for quite some time. I do hope he is alright.

We had a lovely time yesterday. We had dinner with delicious steak and then we drove to the beach. It was beautiful. Did you receive the cards I sent from New Caledonia?

December 19, 1943

I've written so many letters that I'm getting writer's cramp and I still have one to write to Wilber. I hope everyone's well. Is Nonie all right now? I received a letter from Alberta and two of yours since I've been here. The watch hasn't arrived yet.

You did receive the box with Jean's letters, didn't you? I wouldn't want to lose those. Did you renew the subscription on the Reader's Digest? I'm going to send for some more magazines, but I can do that from here. If you can get some of Cara Nome's powdered perfume and some medium panties with elastic, you can send them to me. The clerk in the store before we left said they were going to make some more, and I hate those others, otherwise, I have about everything.

My insurance is due the first of the year if you'll take care of that. Oh yes, did you send a change of address for the R.N.

(Registered Nurse Magazine)? If so, will you change it to the
one that is on my letters now?

Christmas is going to seem so far away this year. Over the
radio you can get some Christmas carols but very few. It's
mostly popular music.

I did my daily mending, washing, etc. today and am trying to
get ahead on writing letters, but I'll never catch up.

How does John Vern like school by now? I do hope he
continues to like it as much as he has.

Is Dad getting any fatter? Does he still go out to the farm
every day? Have a nice Christmas. Are you having the
Christmas dinner? Oh! I don't know whether I ever told you or
not, but Susie Bell married some wealthy lumber man from the
north. Heaven bless her soul. I guess that's it OK.

December 29, 1943

Here it is almost another year—how I do hope it's much
better for everyone concerned—which is everyone—than last
year. I do hope this finds you all well, and that you had a lovely
time at Christmas. I thought of you all and the boys crawling
on the floor playing with the kid's toys and the tree. Was it as
pretty as usual?

We had a lovely time here, but it's a little out of line for
what Christmas should be. I'm enclosing a menu, so you can
see that the chow was especially good.

Have you heard from Jean yet? Gee! I'm worried about him.
He's such a swell person. Write and tell me all the news about
the kids and all the people around there that I knew.

I have a cute green doll. Barbara or Nancy would love it. It is
supposed to be a good luck doll. Otherwise, I'd send it to them.
I've given all my good luck pieces away.

Did Steve send you the camera? I wish now that I had brought it with me, but I didn't have enough room anyway.

I weighed today, and I'm still the same as when I was home on leave, and for once I'm getting enough rest. I'm trying to crochet. I don't know if I'll ever succeed or not.

They passed a new ruling, so I'll have to stay here a year whether I'm married or not. I haven't told Jean yet, but I will in the next letter.

I must close now. Oh! Yes! Dean and Bud are out here somewhere, are they not? If you will send their addresses, I'd appreciate it. Well, if I'm going to get up in the morning to work, I must retire.

Good night, all.

Menu from Christmas dinner December 1943, U.S. Naval Mobile Hospital No. 6

January 2, 1944

I've been wondering what happened to you all since I haven't heard from you for two weeks. The watch hasn't arrived yet, but I'll let you know the minute it arrives.

If I don't get a card to Dad before his birthday, I hope it is a happy one. Eat another piece of cake for me. Also I believe Bobby has one, but I'll send him something because I know he would love to get it.

The horse races finish tomorrow, some of the kids went, but I didn't go because I knew I would bet too much.

How are all the kids? Fine, I hope. Did you celebrate the new year? Is Uncle Calvin any better and has Forest gone into the army yet?

Letter to Jean Showe, her fiancé. He was on the USS Harding based out of New York at the time.

January 5, 1944

Dearest Jean,

You'll never realize how happy I was when I looked in my mailbox and there were thirteen from you. Darling, you can just keep on writing like that I shall never get tired of it, and I love to hear it.

Everything is OK here now, and your hopes are an actuality. There are enough amusements, sports, etcetera to take care of everyone's needs.

I'm actually ashamed to write V-mail but I thought it might reach you sooner than the other.

I miss you so much Jean and think of you constantly. I'm glad the folks wrote to you. I believe I heard from them all and each one told me about the letter. "Tiny" is Mrs. McIntosh.

Mrs. Carson, is also my sister. Mrs. Murphy is the name of the other so that you can keep them straight in case they get you too confused. I sent Wilber the snap of you holding your niece. I don't believe he understood, anyway, I have to write an explanation.

Darling, I love you as much as ever and I shall continue to do so. This can't last forever.

RETURN TO NEW ZEALAND

Esther had been reassigned to New Zealand because her letter to her parents dated January 5, 1944, had "Somewhere in New Zealand" in the heading.

According to a list of ships for transport found in Mom's belongings, she left for her duty station in New Zealand on the USS Crescent City. My information on the Crescent City comes from a publication by The National WWII Museum in New Orleans, Louisiana. USS Crescent City (AP-40/APA-21) like her other ride, the USS Rochambeau, started out as just another cargo vessel built at the Bethlehem Shipbuilding Company in Sparrow's Point, Maryland. Called the Del Orleans, she was built for the Delta line as a coffee hauler and passenger ship to go between the United States and Africa.

The USS Crescent City

She only made one voyage before the U.S. Navy, desperate for ships, took her over in June 1941. She was converted to a troop transport at Alabama Dry Dock and Shipbuilding Company in Mobile, Alabama where she was commissioned in the US Navy on October 10th, 1941, as the USS Crescent City (AP-40). The ship had a crew of 500 and would be able to carry over 1,100 men into combat.

Like the USS Rochambeau, the USS Crescent City made many trips to various ports in California and the Pacific before participating in the Guadalcanal campaign. The Japanese began building an airstrip on Guadalcanal. The island of Guadalcanal occupied a strategic position in the South Pacific near sea lanes that the Allied forces would use to advance on Japan. It was determined by the Allied commanders that the Japanese could not be allowed to build the airfield.

On July 31st, 1942, the Crescent City, along with eighteen other transports, eight cruisers, and twenty-four destroyers, screened by aircraft carriers, set off for the island. The landings began on August 7th, 1942, at Guadalcanal and Tulagi, and initially met very little Japanese resistance. What followed was months of continuous, fierce, and deadly combat in the air, on the sea, and on land.

While the outcome of the battle hung in the balance, the Crescent City made numerous trips to and from the island, delivering desperately needed men and supplies to try to hold off the Japanese from retaking the island. In total, the Crescent City made fourteen trips and brought 7,000 men to Guadalcanal between August 1942 and February 1943. Due to the Crescent City's and other ships' efforts, the U.S. Navy reclassified them to Attack Transports (APA) to differentiate them from standard cargo carriers and to reflect their status as transports that took part in the assault landings themselves. The Crescent City took part in the assault on Bougainville and conducted follow up supply runs during November 1943 through February 1944.

She then took part in the assault landings in Guam in July 1944, carrying men of the 3rd Marine Division, and served as a floating hospital treating wounded men. She landed men from the famous 1st Marine Regiment of the 1st Marine Division, again serving as a floating hospital offshore treating men from the devastating battle on the island. She participated in the landings on Leyte in the Philippines in October 1944 and after an overhaul, joined in the assault on Okinawa.

Throughout the war, the Crescent City would shoot down eight Japanese planes, earn ten Battle Stars, and serve as a flagship for three major amphibious assaults. She served from Guadalcanal through Okinawa and spent more time in a combat area than any other transport in the US Navy. Crescent City also traveled 160,000 miles and transported 90,000 men. Amazingly, even though she was in the thick of the fight, the ship was never damaged.

U.S. NAVAL MOBILE HOSPITAL NO. 6, WELLINGTON, NEW ZEALAND

The information about how U.S. Naval Hospital No. 6, Esther's second duty station in the Pacific, was established was obtained from the Victoria University of Wellington Library, New Zealand Electronic Text Collection, XIII: Medical Services in New Zealand and the Pacific. More detailed information about the hospital in WWII was abstracted from an article in Corpus, a forum for conversations about medicine and life. The article, titled "Silverstream Hospital and the Marines," was taken from an address given by Susanna (Susi) Williams, who was the Medical Superintendent of Silverstream Hospital from 1982-1989.

Japanese military successes in early 1942, especially the fall of Singapore, made the possibility of an invasion of New Zealand very real. There was an arrangement in place with the government of New Zealand for U.S. troops to be stationed there. In exchange, the

U.S. was able to use New Zealand as a base for operations in the Southwest Pacific.

In June of 1942, troops from the 37th Division, U.S. Army and First Marine Division, United States Marine Corps, arrived in New Zealand. With U.S. troops stationed there, the country would be safer, their troops could remain in North Africa, with New Zealand serving as a base for American operations against Japanese-occupied islands in the South Pacific.

Considerable liaison was carried out by the medical staff of New Zealand Army Headquarters with the administrative medical officers of the American Division, with a view to assisting them in the organization of their medical arrangements. The U.S. medical units agreed to assist in the supply of much-needed drugs and other medical equipment.

The New Zealand government had started construction of the Silverstream Hospital, fifteen miles north of Wellington, in 1941. In May 1942, as the hospital was nearing completion, the decision was made to increase its size and hand it over to the recently arrived U.S. Navy. U.S. Navy Mobile Hospital No. 6 occupied the Silverstream site from August 1942 until April 1944.

The Americans used the hospital to treat malaria victims, the wounded from the War in the Pacific, and sick soldiers from the First Marine Division, who were camped around the greater Wellington area. Approximately 20,000 patients were treated there from 1942 to 1944. At its peak, the hospital was able to accommodate 1,600 patients.

The nurses were American. Mom remembered living in the Nurses Home that was secured with Marine guards and barbed wire. Many of the cases at the hospital were Marines with cerebral malaria. The treatment was bitter tasting quinine. This is where Esther was probably served baked beans on toast for breakfast. She was not fond of this British breakfast staple. Decades later, I phoned her after finding it at a London hotel breakfast buffet and we had a good laugh about it.

After the hospital was no longer needed, Wellington Hospital Board took it over.

TROPICAL DISEASES

My information on the other foe Esther faced in the South Pacific was provided by a government website called the AMEDD Center of History and Heritage. AMEDD is an acronym for the U.S. Army Medical Corps. According to Chapter VIII of the AMEDD Center, malaria was the single most serious health hazard to Allied troops in the South Pacific Area during WWII. It caused five times as many casualties as did combat. It is estimated that more than 100,000 individuals among Allied personnel contracted malaria in the South Pacific. Malaria threatened the success of the military campaigns on Guadalcanal and Solomon Islands.

Other tropical diseases such as dengue fever, filariasis, tsutsug-mushi disease, and w. barcrofti microfilariae were problems as well. When I was about five years old, I remember my father having a nasty-looking green fungus-like skin condition on his shins that came from his time in the South Pacific. My father said the various skin diseases encountered were called "jungle rot" by the allied forces. Dad's fungus cleared up after a couple of years. I don't remember him being troubled by it after that.

Excerpts from Esther's letter to her parents

January 5, 1944

I received about four letters from you yesterday all written
to my old address, nevertheless it was good to hear from you. I
think it's wonderful that my letters are coming through so fast.
Neither the Christmas box, nor the watch have arrived as of
yet, but if it took the letters this long, the packages are probably
still on their way.

I received several letters from Wilber and shall see if I can't
forward them on. The most recent letter was written December
the 5th, also a Christmas card with some foreign language
which I was unable to understand. There were thirteen letters
from Jean which made me feel much better. He said that he was
going to write you. I don't know exactly when you will get the
letter.

I'm trying to get a tan on my legs and face. Here's hoping I
succeed. I miscounted, there were ten letters. They were dated
December 10th, December 13th, October 10th, November
29th, December 17th, December 3rd, November 23rd,
November 5th, November 19th and December 16th. You knew
of course that the above address is the one we were using now.
I was really mad when I didn't hear from you and decided I
wouldn't write until I had heard.

Excerpts from a letter to her sister Alberta Murphy and family

January 7, 1944

That snow really sounds good. I received a letter from Jean
telling me he had written to Tiny. Is she still at home? I also

received your letter of December 12th. I get my routine correspondence finished and then I'm tired.

I've been reading a great deal especially those by Kenneth
Roberts. "Arundel" and "The Lively Lady." It is wonderful to sit
down and read once more. I'm enclosing a letter from Wilber. I
thought you might enjoy it. I've wondered how long it takes
letters from here to go to him.

Do you still have the Pla-Mor? (Author's note: an abbreviation for Play More, this was a neighborhood club for playing
games and socializing). I thought they had disbanded long ago.
Is it still the same old gang?

We went to the show the other night, but it was Lupe Velez
in something or other, we couldn't take it so left in the middle
of it. I received my clean shirts today, but I'm still shining
shoes, washing, and ironing. Golly! I'm really going to be good.
I guess I was really lazy before.

I wondered if Bob's eye has changed back to its normal
color. And how is Barbara? Does Verda's boyfriend live around
there? I did so want to see George L., Priscilla, and the rest in
San Diego but I didn't have time. Is Harry still in Clay or did he
finally have to go in the army?

Had a letter from Steve, Johnny, Leota, and the rest
(Author's note: these were friends of Mom's she met in nurse's
training in Missouri). Do you remember Johnny when she was
home the first time? She's not the same person. In fact she
advised me to get married—me of all people.

Golly! Tell Bill (her sister's husband) to save some fishing
lines because I'm going when I get back. Maybe we'll get by this
time without practically drowning half the family.

Photo of a street in New Zealand

Letters to her parents

January 8, 1944

While waiting for one of the girls to get ready to go to town I'll dash off a few lines. The watch or Christmas boxes have neither one arrived. Jean said he sent a book, and it hasn't arrived, but in spite of everything I'm doing very well. I haven't lost the six pounds that I've gained since I arrived in the Navy. I still want to gain five more pounds but haven't succeeded as yet.

We're going to town to see if we can't locate a wastepaper basket. I really doubt if we'll be lucky but at least we can try.

I had a lovely card from Mrs. Paro. She enclosed two snaps which were very good. Also heard from Jean. It'll probably be some while before I'll hear again. I'm running out of patience—but I guess I'll have to be content.

We're going horseback riding next week. It's been so long since I've been on a horse that I don't know if I can still ride one. They say they have a good learner, meaning a horse that won't dash off with you.

I would have loved to see the kids at Christmas. I'll bet they were absolutely precious. Do Nancy or Barbara have curly hair? I really don't know where they get it from.

January 15, 1944

I just finished breakfast and thought I would drop you a line. I made my own this morning as I had strawberries which were purchased yesterday. We did some shopping yesterday. I found the prettiest mohair rug but when I use their money I never know until I get home how much I pay for the thing. I found Bobby a birthday card, but I couldn't find any for Dad that were suitable, so I'll just wish him a happy birthday.

Next day—I had the most pleasant surprise when I came off duty. There were four letters from you dated December 20th, December 31st, December 6th, and November 8th. It was really grand to hear from you. I haven't as yet received either the box or the watch—and I was so mad the other night because someone borrowed my shirt and forgot to return it. I really don't care if they needed it badly.

I can just see John Vern sliding along on the ice. Didn't you go to Jean's (Author's note: likely one of her cousins) reception? How many are there left now? Can't be too many? Apparently, you aren't getting all my letters because I've really written more than you had in your letter.

Yes, I knew Elmo, but I'm afraid unless they come down this way, I shan't see them. How long has Elmo been out here?

I'm sorry to hear about Verda, but glad that she's back to

work. Who was the nurse that was in my class? Did she tell them her name? Most, in fact all but Winnie, are now married. Oh! Golly—I forgot myself.

I haven't been to the movies lately. The pictures are all a little old.

You should have by now received my first allotment. If not, you should receive it sometime this month.

We alternate A.M. and P.M. duty so some weeks I work in the morning and others in the afternoon. I must close now and answer some more letters. We're still getting Christmas cards. Write when you find time.

~

January 18, 1944

I received the watch today, and it's lovely, thank you ever so much. I'll write to all the other kids too. I also received the other box. I don't know how you knew what I needed but it was just right.

I'm writing this sitting up in bed, so if you can't read it, you'll understand why. You should be getting my letters much sooner now than you did before. Before I forget it, thank Mrs. Bloom for me. The soap is really divine. It smells so good.

I'd love to see Nancy with her dog that must really be cute. Why does dad like collies so well?

I haven't heard from Wilber except for the one letter he had addressed to Mare Island. I sent you it though. I'm going to try and write him tonight if I don't get too sleepy.

Dad, you gave us the wrong problems you should have made them in English money. But it's not too bad.

We went to town today especially to get my alarm clock. It's been there a month now. It seems that he just got back from a vacation and hasn't had time. Golly! Was I ever mad.

I wanted to let you know that I had received the watch and to thank you again.

~

Birthday card to Esther's nephew Robert Murphy

January 27, 1944

Bobby, how are you by now? I suppose the eye is cured. It didn't hurt too much, did it? I'm sorry I missed your birthday but maybe next year I will be there. Are you still drinking your milk?
Love,
Aunt Esther

~

Excerpts from letters to her sister, Alberta Murphy and family

January 27, 1944

Tell Bobby I'm sorry but I just can't write him a letter on this paper (V-mail). I did send him a birthday card that I found downtown.
I'm glad for Imogene. I hope she is doing nicely or as they say here, "Both well." Is Tiny still at home? Gee! I finally received the watch and it's a honey. I'd almost given up hope.
If you see Mrs. Abels, tell her hello for me. Gee! She certainly has had a tough time of it. Why don't Rose and Imogene's mothers speak? I had a lovely letter and some snaps from Mrs. Paro.
Not much has happened except that we've gone horseback riding several times. As far as the hours we work are concerned,

they are the same as back in the States. Here it is the bottom of the sheet. I also got your Christmas card.

February 5, 1944

I was too lazy to dress for chow, so I fried myself some bacon—had a bacon and tomato sandwich, some apricots and coffee. the coffee was delicious and decided to write some more letters. I'm almost caught up. Tomorrow, I don't have to work so I'm house cleaning, mending and polishing shoes—such is life.

Really aren't you afraid their stock of mirrors might give out pretty soon? Where are Jean and Orville going to live? Did the folks go to the reception? It doesn't seem like Barbara is old enough to have teeth. Time passes so quickly. It will soon be a year since Tiny was married. I'm sending Bobby a folder. I hope he likes it. Poor Rhea, she must have an awful time—by the way what happened to Ralph?

Everything is fine here. We now have roses, carnations, etcetera in our quarters. Flowers certainly help a place. We also have a lovely fireplace. On rainy nights, we start the fire, listen to the radio, read or write letters, or whatever one is inclined to do. We have movies three nights a week where you can go downtown, but downtown you are like a jack-in-the-box. First down and then up. The pictures are all a little old, but I haven't seen some of them.

Belongings that Esther held onto: A Navy belt, two carved heads, a tiki, and a Pearl Harbor pin

I went shopping yesterday. It is fun watching the people—I still like them and think they're interesting. These of course are a little different and the first question they'll ask you is how you like the place. The women all carry little woven baskets to do their shopping in. They don't hold much so I can't see any reason for carrying it. I purchased a black wooden box, supposedly hand carved and two tikis, which are really horrible looking things.

Francis gave me her handkerchief dress when I came out as I didn't have time to make mine. They are cute with white shirts and are easy to make (cheap too). All you have to have is five large bandana handkerchiefs. Three for the skirt, and the top is cut out of the handkerchief. Launders easily too.

I'm now wearing glasses again. I hope this clears my eyes up. It's disgusting to have someone always asking you if you've been on a week's drunk or crying.

I haven't heard from Jean since I received the last batch of

95

letters. His mother will let me know if he isn't all right, so I don't worry as much as I used to.

I know it's a little early but are you doing anything for the folks on their wedding anniversary? The way I have it figured it's their 36th. If so count me in, and I will send the money to you by money order. I must close and write some more.

Letters to her parents

February 15, 1944

Hope this finds you all well and not freezing. Have you had any more snow? Do you know I forgot all about Bobby's birthday? Would you get something for me and send it to him? There isn't much here that you can't get there so you might as well send it from there.

What color is the linoleum that you have in the kitchen? Is it inlaid or just plain? Did you ever get the blanket for me? I haven't heard from Jean for ages, but I don't expect to, very often so then it isn't so bad.

My alarm clock went on the blink, so I've been sleeping with one eye shut and the other open. Next week I have P.M. duty so I can sleep later. The watch is grand and so is the eversharp (Author's note: probably a pen or pencil with retractable lead). I received the Reader's Digest but not the R.N. (Registered Nurse magazine).

I just finished a long letter to Steve. Did she send the camera home? I didn't realize that I was spread from one end of the state to the other.

I finally received my glasses and sincerely hope that they do the work. They aren't so bad for foreign glasses.

How is Verda? Have you heard lately? "Red" Young is the one I was referring to but he's probably further up north.

I purchased a hand carved box yesterday. It is really a pretty one. Also a few tikis. I still have to ride a tram. I think it would be fun, although they're forever and a day running into each other.

Not much of interest has happened lately. Have you heard from Wilber? I must sign off and get myself cleaned up.

Letter to her sister, Alberta Murphy and family

February 16, 1944

I received your January 12th letter. It's not necessary to tell you that it was good to hear from you. I'm glad for Wilber. It will be a reprieve from what he'll probably have to do.

I wish I could have joined you all at the birthday dinner. In Johnny's last letter, her husband is going into the Army and her brother was reported missing. Poor kid. She really has had her share.

I'm afraid you'll have to look the weather up. It is a forbidden subject, and the censor would cut it out.

I received three letters from Jean today. He had a three day leave and went home—Jeepers! It makes me mad when I stop to think. Mail comes through fairly well now. Once in a while it seems slow, but it really isn't.

Our living quarters are comfortable. I'm going to try and borrow a camera and take the quarters. I must close now as it's the bottom and I have so many to write.

Letter to her parents

March 7, 1944

I received your February 22nd and February 23rd V-mail letters. Also, your January 14th, February 18th and your February 14th letter. It was good to hear from you. I also had a letter from Verda and she is back to work and also one from Jean's mother. Mail has been pretty good lately. I'm enclosing one of Wilber's letters. I received it quite some time ago but thought you would enjoy it just the same.

We spent Sunday at the beach. It was really lovely. I bought some books for John Vern and Bobby. Do you think they would like some seashells too? I received the picture of Nancy, Bobby and Barbara and they all look darling.

The eversharp and candy bars came through in good shape. Also the brownies arrived but they were moldy so of course couldn't be eaten. The perfumed powder will probably take some time. I received a box of soap from Frisco yesterday. It was from the girl whom we specialed. (Author's note: she probably means sponsored or mentored in some way.) I also received a box of "Evening in Paris" powder. They eventually catch up with us. I wrote Arlene a letter, but I guess it hasn't arrived as yet.

I finally had my radio fixed. I really missed it when it was on the blink. I decided against buying too many bonds. Just one $50 a month. I came to that conclusion after arriving here, so the others you bought me are all right. Thanks for taking care of all those wedding presents, etcetera for me. I really appreciate it and it's all right to take as much money as you need.

Verda said that Steve had been sick. I meant to send her a card but as usual I'm late.

I met a Davis who knew Bill, Elton, and Mary Evelyn. I can't remember if he's a fraternity brother or not, but he knew them at Topeka. Also L. Henry. I just can't place him, but I believe he used to go with Tiny, didn't he? Anyway, we had a milkshake and talked over old times. It was good to see someone who knew someone you did.

I haven't had a letter from Jean for about two weeks, but I'm sure he's out again. Is Nonie's new address Longford? I have the darndest time with them.

My roommate's roommate who was at Mare Island is now here. We all took in an Army dance the other night. It was fun but the music was horrible.

My foot is all right now—No! I didn't injure it. It was only a corn, but it hurt like the devil. I really must close now, or I won't be able to get both letters in.

February 28, 1944

Hope this finds you all well. It has been several days since I received a letter from you. Everything is lovely here—I was wishing Dad could have been along this morning.

We went to the racetrack and watched them groom some of the horses for the races tomorrow. They were really beautiful creatures and not the least bit scared of us. One of the girls is going to ride it someday. They asked us over for dinner sometime next week.

Sunday, we spent the day at the beach, and you should see us. We came back with sand in our hair clothes, etc. and our faces a little sunburned.

I was happy to hear that that Dean and Merle were both back. I received a letter from Wilber and will enclose it in the next one I write. I must close now.

Letters to her sister, Alberta Murphy and family

March 9, 1944

I have to stay in this afternoon so might as well dash off a few lines. I just this minute—1600, I received two V-mails from you. One was dated February 13th, the other February 28th, so it only took the last one ten days to get here. I hope Bill (her sister Alberta's husband) had a happy birthday. I know I'm a little late but better late than never.

Thanks for the pictures, I really don't think Barbara looks like anyone. I sent all my letters from Wilber home so that you can read them too.

I met a kid who knew the Macintoshes (Author's note: Esther's brother-in-law's family; her sister Lavonne was married to Bill MacIntosh). He said he knew Elton better than Bill and he also knew Mary Evelyn. He graduated from Washburn—law. We spent the evening together talking over old times.

Bill the flyer is going to get to go home. I'm so happy for him that I think I'll celebrate too. He's a wonderful dancer and can really get around on the dance floor. He thought he was going to get to come down here for a few days.

I certainly wish the darn flies would go away and leave me in peace. I had to bring someone's laundry off the line before they had to do it over.

I haven't had a letter from Jean for almost two weeks. I really don't expect one for another two or three weeks. I really miss him.

We went to the beach last Sunday. You would have loved it. The houses are right next to the beach with a few yards of sand between the houses and water. The tide was in at the time we were there, and quite a few people were in swimming. We gathered shells all afternoon and my nose turned a little red but it's back to its normal color again.

I love to hear about the children so write and tell me all about them. I'm glad you can talk to Nonie over the telephone. How far are their nearest neighbors?

I have some books for the boys but haven't gotten around to mailing them yet. I'm so hungry I think I'll get ready for chow. Write when you find the time.

Letters to her parents

March 16, 1944

I thought I would write on paper once, so dad could be sure and read it. I'll only have time for a short note as it's almost time to go to work. I'm working P.M.'s this week so I get to sleep late; this morning though, I was up before 9:00 A.M. I went to town to buy some stationery and I forgot it, so I got this at our Ship's Service—ain't it awful?

It is now 11:00 PM and I finished today's work, ate chow, and spent one hour shining shoes and washing my hair and then I talked myself into writing some letters. The chow wasn't bad tonight. Altogether it's been a grand day—no reference to the weather. I was thinking of you Mother and your bucket to catch rainwater to wash hair. I'll soon have enough.

I had a letter from Jean, day before yesterday. He was grand, gaining weight and feeling fine. He sent his love.

I intend to send Mrs. Bloom the folder, but I don't know her address. I will send it anyway.

I will send you a money order to get Nancy something for her birthday. I can't find anything over here that you can't get there.

I've received the Reader's Digest swell, but I've never received the R.N. When we get them, they're usually about a month old but we enjoy them just the same.

I received the picture of Nancy and wrote to Arlene. Maybe she hadn't received the letter yet.

Continued March 17th, 1944. Today is Saint Patrick's Day. How time does fly. I didn't get up until 11:30 today, and since the maid is cleaning my room and the painter is painting the radiator, I haven't been there since. We got our own breakfast and read the morning newspaper and then pressed a uniform—and now it's again time to go to work.

April 15, 1944

Please excuse the paper, as it is all I can find. I received your March 21st, March 17th, 28th, 24th, and April the 1st letters, and as usual it was good to hear from you.

We had a few days off and took a little trip, it was wonderful. On Sunday morning we decided to go, and by Monday we were ready. All we could get were second class accommodations on the train, but we were soon in first class. It took us six hours to arrive at our destinations.

Not having any hotel accommodations, we had to hurry around and obtain some. We ended up in the best hotel in town. (Eleanor was a guest there.) (Author's note: that would be Eleanor Roosevelt when she was doing a Red Cross tour of the South Pacific.).

We cleaned up for dinner, and after having coffee in the lounge, we went to a movie called "Happy Go Lucky." It was really good and kept us in stitches all the way through. After the movie we went home and retired early.

Next morning early, we were awakened for tea by the maid, if you can imagine anyone having tea in bed. We were up soon after and down in the lobby before breakfast was announced.

That was the last time we made that mistake. They announce it by banging on dish pans.

After breakfast, we took a bus out into the country to meet the Maori guide. As usual we were about an hour early, so we shopped and purchased some postal cards. You also should expect a package soon.

Rangi soon arrived and showed us through this village. We crossed a bridge over a clear stream into a regular steam bath. The people that live there use the steam for cooking, bathing, washing clothes, etcetera, also for heating their houses. The guide put some corn in to cook before we started around. When we returned, she said it would be cooked.

One girl was taking her four-month-old baby out in an open pool, another was washing her hair, and still another was doing her family washing. They had some bread on to cook as many of the places are really hot. There were two geysers, very playful and they really acted up the day we were there. I must close now. Is the river out again? (Author's note: I believe she is asking if there is flooding in town.)

Write when you have time.

Letter to her sister, Alberta Murphy and family

April 19, 1944

I received a letter from you yesterday and was glad to hear. I also received one from Nonie—she must be pretty well settled by now. There was one from Jean too, so it was a pretty good day.

I would love to see Bobby's room. It sounds as though he should be proud of it. Oh! Yes—I had a letter from Steve. She's been ill apparently, she ate a hamburger which didn't agree with her. She's back at work now after a rest at home.

I'm fine except for a cold, flea bites, and a little stiff from horseback riding.

We visited a Maori village and enjoyed it very much. They had some geysers which happened to be active at the time we were there, (similar to Yellowstone National Park). It is a volcanic region, steam comes out of the earth at several spots and they never know where it will appear.

The natives (Maori) use the steam to cook, bathe, bake, wash, etc. They were bathing a four-month-old baby out in this open pool. He didn't cry or anything, and I was thinking of all the precautions we take with our four-month-old babies.

I understand the postage rates have gone up it doesn't seem possible—but I understand it's true.

We took in the horse races a week ago. I lost a pound and a half approximately $5. Mother said that she had a letter from Donald L. How on earth they can ever use him is more than I can see? They really must be desperate for men.

Maori children, New Zealand

I'm glad Bobby liked the sweater and colors. I'm sorry I was late—but better late than never.

I received a letter from Edwina and Bob thanking me for my part in the mirror. She really must have liked it. I haven't answered it yet as I'm way behind again.

Must sign off until next time. Write if you can find time when not watching your two kids. By the way, Francisco is spelled like I have written it. It hurt some of the Frisco's authentic sons to spell it the other way and they told me to be sure and tell you.

Letter from Esther's brother Wilber in the Army in England

April 23, 1944

Hello Sailor,

How's the Navy doing in New Zealand? I received your March 22 letter a few days ago, and as usual, it took about a week for your turn to come. One of these days I'm going to surprise myself and catch up on my letter writing.

You're telling me the tea drinkers like to talk. The other night a little fellow with a glass eye got me cornered and it took me a whole hour to get away. He was an old, but rather snappy dresser, man with a derby and a very devoted pet dog. He had spent most of his years in the service of the British Empire as an engineer. From the way he talked, he had been all over the world a couple of times and was especially proud of his ability to speak French. That's what took so long, he'd tell a story in French and then have to translate it into English so we could understand it. It wouldn't have been so bad listening to him except that he kept pulling out his glass eye and putting it back the wrong way which gave him a sort of a cross eyed effect. Gosh what characters a fellow can run into.

Say, you know that book you sent me in the Christmas box? Well, it has created a slight disturbance around here. The book lay in my locker for quite some time until Horn was hunting for something to read, and I let him have it.

"What a guy. What a guy," he kept saying after finishing it. So, I read the thing, everybody in this barracks read it, and at present it is making the rounds in the next one. Boy, what a Romeo that newspaper man was—he could seduce more women in a week than an average man in a lifetime. If you happen to run onto anymore stories like that one, send them along we all enjoy them.

Love,

John Wilber

Letters to her parents

April 27, 1944

I received your April 15th letter today and I have your April 8th and 4th. Also had a letter from Homer Nauman. He said he liked his duty real, well. I was surprised to hear from him.

Had a letter from Steve and she's been ill, but she said that she'd send the camera. She'll take good care of it. Also heard from Verda and she's back at work and feeling better. I'm glad Mrs. Blume liked the cards in spite of the fact that I had her name all fouled up and the address was way off. Give her my regards.

The best of all though was your letter and one from Jean. He was at home again. Lucky him! As for the place you mentioned, you can see I'm not there by the heading of my letter. It would be too good to even be true if I could just see Jean. I have some snaps to send to you as soon as we have them finished.

A friend of Bill's stopped by yesterday to tell me that he was at home safe and sound. It was such good news that I was happy to see him.

On our leave, we visited some Hot Springs. The native Maories cook, wash, and use it for their heating system. The guide put some corn in to boil before we started on a tour. We visited some geysers and saw the carvings done by some of the natives. We have pictures of them which we took. We saw boiling mud, which was to me the most interesting as it really must be hot for mud to boil.

When we arrived back in the forenoon, the corn was well done. We had a little butter even though it's rationed, and it tasted good. In the afternoon, we took a trip to some more hot springs with steam and boiling mud. Steve, while taking some pictures stepped into the pool, but it didn't hurt him.

Hot Springs in Rotorua, New Zealand

Gee! I would love to see the kids. They must be cute and ornery. John Verne's school should be up about now, shouldn't it?

The reason I didn't write for such a long time was because I ran out of paper and didn't get downtown in time to get any.

We have a new radio program with US plays, music, announcers, and news, and it really sounds good. We attended a basketball game downtown the other night. The score was 27 to 21 and it was really exciting.

Hope this finds you all well and happy. I have so many letters to write that I must close.

Write soon.

Letter to her sister, Alberta Murphy and family

April 27, 1944

Before me I have your March 15th, 31st and April 9th letters. There was quite a bit of mail today, so everyone is happy. I heard from Homer N., the folks, Steve, and Jean. Several others from kids you wouldn't know.

I've become quite an expert at making fudge, because when I can't find anything else to do, I make some fudge and I have it down to a fine art.

We attended a program similar to our radio Doctor I.Q. at home, only this one was named Doctor G.I. The JG (Author's note: Likely stands for Lieutenant Junior Grade) that I was with was asked the question (for a carton of cigarettes). It was fun and I never laughed so much.

You can tell Bobby that we saw mud boiling. It bubbled up in fantastic shapes, and we saw fish in a pool of water that were much larger than any he ever caught.

I'm glad that Tiny can be with Bill. He should be completing his training soon, shouldn't he?

Homer seemed to like it very much where he's at. He's been over about six months.

I must close now as I have several more letters to write. Hope this finds you all well and happy. Can Barbara walk yet?

Letter to her parents

May 15, 1944

Received two letters from you dated April 29th and May 2nd and it was good to hear from you. Also had a letter from Wilber. It's too bad about Nancy's birthday party. The roads really must be rugged.

Bebe and I saw their famous glow worm grotto over the weekend. It is about 100 miles from our station. We drove up in a Jeep. It took us about four hours as the roads are very winding, we didn't make such good time and we also stopped for lunch.

It is in rather a deserted part of the country, but they have a large hotel, and as usual, no heat except the fireplace. It was very informal as everyone would crowd around the fireplace and knit, play cards, et cetera. We played a game of progressive ping pong. What a game.

That night the guide took about ten of us through this glow worm grotto. It is a cave with stalactites hanging from the wall. I don't believe the cave part is as pretty as The Cave of the Winds, but the next trip, we entered by boat and travelled along this underground river. No lights and noise were advisable as the glow worms extinguish their light at the least disturbance. A more wonderful sight you could not hope to see. It looked like a black velvet background with millions of sparkling jewels placed up on it. In several places, the glow made such a light that it was like a moonlit night.

We visited the caves, but they only had formations which are very old, but as I'm not a geologist, they were not as interesting.

How are all the kids? I haven't heard from Jean, but he told me not to expect to hear for some time. Arlene sent me some snapshots of all the kids taken when Lavonne was at home.

I'm like Wilber, just a little behind in answering my letters,

but I'll catch up someday. Well, it's almost chow time. I'll have
to dash along.

Letter to her sister, Alberta Murphy and family

May 16, 1944

Received your April 28th V-mail yesterday. Makes it 12 days.
Not bad I'd say. You are welcome for the correction. One of the
corpsmen from Frisco noticed it.

We get a great deal of time to ourselves because when we
are finished with our work our time is our own to a certain
degree. As usual there are a lot of rules and regulations.
Someday again I'm going to wear what I please.

How is Bob's eye? I hope nothing happens to it as eyes to
me are a delicate subject. I mailed some books for him so he
should get them soon.

I think we are leaving sometime in the future. I don't know
where we're going but we're off again. So, if the folks don't hear
for some time, don't let them worry.

We saw the stage play "Susan and God" last night and it was
wonderful. Maybe it was the idea of a stage play.

Had several letters from Jean several days ago. He apparently isn't getting mine. He was looking for a house the last
time he was home. Jeepers! If you kids couldn't keep house
without Mom, what am I going to do?

Between your two problem children, write me anytime you
find time.

Letter to her parents

May 20, 1944

I'm dashing this off rather hurriedly so if you can't read it you will understand, but I wanted you to write to the following address: U.S.N. Base hospital #6 in care of San Francisco California. The rest is the same.

Hope this finds you all well as I know it will. The weather must be awful hot there now, as I understand it was very hot in New York. I just finished two nights of night duty and with washing, ironing, and what have you, I haven't written much.

Received a letter from you yesterday with Tiny's change of address. Thanks a lot. I really haven't written to her yet, but I will sometime.

Jean is in school for six weeks and then he will probably go to a hospital. So, I might see him sometime soon. Glad you enjoyed the letter. Will write more later.

NEW HEBRIDES, ESPIRITU SANTO

Sketch of Esther by unknown artist, New Hebrides

Esther's next duty station was U.S. Naval Base Hospital No. 6 in Espiritu Santo, New Hebrides. I was able to determine this because it was her duty station on her request to leave the Navy.

Her ride to the New Hebrides was the USS Pinkney. Per Wikipedia, USS Pinkney (APH-2) was a Tryon-class evacuation transport, assigned to the U.S. Navy during WWII. Pinkney served in the Pacific Ocean theater of operations and returned home safely with six battle stars. She was built by Moore Dry Dock in Oakland, California. After Pearl Harbor, she was renamed Pinkney and acquired by the U.S. Navy November 27th, 1942.

USS Pinkney

She departed for the South Pacific in 1943, arriving at Espiritu Santo, then going on to Purvis Bay to the veteran units of the fight for Tulagi and Gavutu to deliver reinforcements and replacements.

Like Esther's other rides, the Pinkney brought men, food, and ammunition forward and evacuated casualties from field hospitals to better facilities on New Caledonia and New Zealand. She also transported American and New Zealand nurses to and between various southwest Pacific hospitals.

During the Okinawa campaign in 1945, she was struck by a kamikaze that damaged the Pinkney and killed eighteen of her crew.

THE NEW HEBRIDES

My Information on the New Hebrides in WWII comes from the World War II database I New Hebrides in WWII. By the eighteenth century, the island group was colonized by both the British and the French. In 1906, the two European powers agreed to share the island group. Britain and France both appointed one resident to oversee the administration of the New Hebrides, each with equal power to enforce the law of their respective countries. The British set up their capital at Hog Harbor, while the French ruled from Segond.

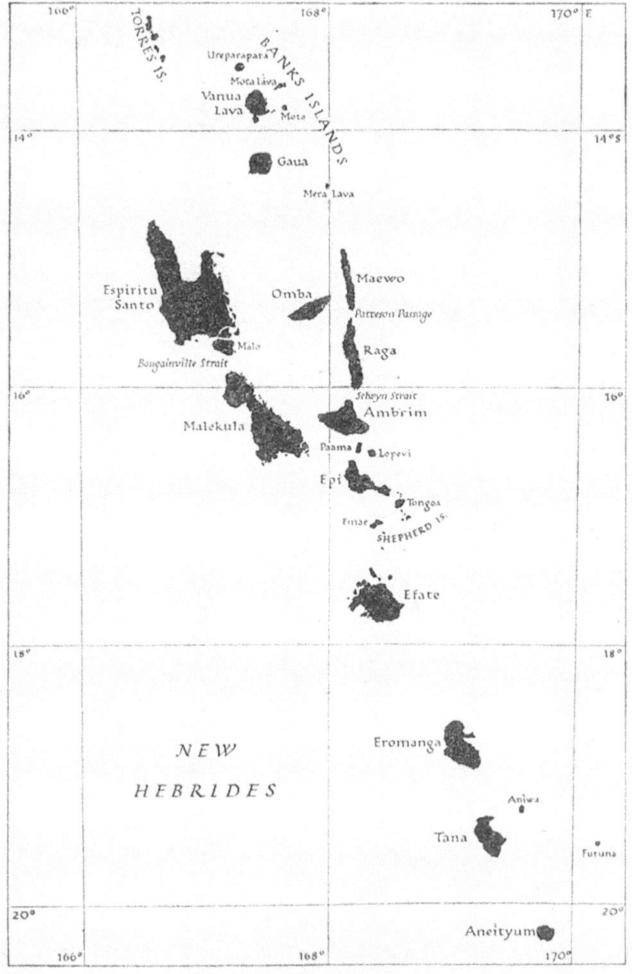

Fig. 165. The New Hebrides
Based on G.S.G.S. map no. 4298 (on a conical projection).

Map of New Hebrides, 1943

With France defeated by Germany in 1940, the French resident, now answering to a non-belligerent Vichy government, lost influence over the course of the war. The British resident allowed the

Australian military in 1941 to establish the New Hebrides Defense Force based on the island of Malekula.

When the Pacific War began in December 1941, because of New Hebrides' strategic location between Australia and the United States, and later the proximity to the Solomon Islands, the islands of Espiritu Santo, Efate, and others in the island group became important military bases for the Allied war effort, hosting airfields and naval anchorages.

After the war, Britain and France, continued to administer the New Hebrides until 1980 when the islands were given independence, forming the new republic of Vanuatu.

ESPIRITU SANTO

Espiritu Santo Naval Advance Base, or Espiritu Santo Naval Base, was most often called just Espiritu Santo (Wikipedia). It was an advance Naval base the U.S. Navy Seabees built during WWII to support the allied effort in the Pacific. The base also supported the U.S. Army and the Army Air Corps, U.S. Coast Guard, and the U.S. Marine Corps. It was the first large advance base built in the Pacific.

Bob Hope arriving at Espiritu Santo Naval Base, New Hebrides
1944

By the end of the war, it was the second-largest base in the South Pacific theater. Its purpose was to repair and resupply ships in theater rather than have them return to the United States. Prior to December 7th, 1941, Pearl Harbor was the largest advance base in the Pacific. Espiritu became capable of all aspects necessary to support the Fleet's operations from Fleet logistics in fuel, food, and ammunition, to transport for combat operations or returning to the United States.

The ship repair facilities and dry docks could attend to most damage and routine maintenance. Without it, ships would have had to travel to Pearl Harbor, Brisbane, or Sydney for major repairs and resupply. The base was also a major rest and relaxation (R&R) destination for the fleet. The build-up of Espiritu Santo was both a defensive strategy and then a staging point for the offense against the Japanese.

The base supported action in the Solomon Islands and Papua, New Guinea. By the end of the war, nine million tons of equipment had been shipped there and over 500,000 servicemen and women had spent time at New Hebrides and Espiritu Santo

THE LASH UP NEWSLETTER FROM NAVAL BASE HOSPITAL NO. 6

Editorial: Morale

Not infrequently our home magazines print tidbits on morale. There was quite a squawk about—the morale building powers of the Vargas gals—when some of Esquire was held up. That is just plain hooey. The best the pin up gals ever did was to give some lads goofy daydreams and a guilty wistful yen for the flesh pots of Egypt and elsewhere.

Movies and the occasional shows furnish entertainment and pleasant distraction from the monotony of an all too humdrum life behind the actual zones of combat. War is always monotonous except during the activity of battle.

But good "morale" is not a matter of entertainment. It is founded on the conviction that we are fighting a just war against evil powers which have upset the peace of the world, bringing a train of suffering and death to many people. We are sharing in the struggle to blot out the ambitious pride and greed for power and military aggrandizement that has caused the worldwide upheaval.

We have a duty to our country, to ourselves and human decency, to perform our part in this struggle as best we can. A realization of our duty coupled with a common sense understanding of the fact, that circumstances, the fortunes of war have made it necessary that we sacrifice, for a time, our normal life in the pleasant surroundings of home, family, and friends. We naturally do not like the separation from those dear to us but, it's part of our job.

Selfishness and self-pity cause poor morale. A manly cause produces the sensible realization that this duty entails certain privations, a sense of humor to grin about our difficulties creates good morale.

The movies, shows, et cetera, are just pleasant doodads to break up the monotony of war.

Under the Rug

At last, I'm really able to open up and give you the word on this place, so stand clear while I beat my gums or you're liable to get splashed with salt water.

I'm on a coral rock in the South Pacific. The island literally swarms with the largest variety of tropical insects you have ever seen, which live in a dense, almost impenetrable jungle.

In fact, everything in this "Lash Up" is different from anything I've ever been used to. For instance, just the other night, while I was attending a wild pig BBQ, I glanced down and saw a hard-shelled bug about one inch long with phosphorescent green running lights 1/8 inch in diameter. There are thousands of ants and lizards everywhere. And boy, can they eat the meat out of the beautifully colored seashells I find on the beach.

For entertainment, we have a movie every night with an occasional USO show for variety. But on beautiful moonlight nights when it isn't raining, I like to go to one of the several outdoor theaters which are usually built in a grove of coconut trees, and on other clear nights it's fun to visit any of the many tree-fringed inlets on the beach and watch the waves and the ocean in the weird light of the Southern Cross or a beautiful, big, tropical moon. Oh man if I only had my honey, could we "pitch the woo."

Fortunately, we normally get every seventh day off, and there are quite a variety of activities to occupy this leisure time. We have baseball, ping pong, touch football, volleyball, badminton, boxing, and horseshoe facilities here at our own camp; in the waters adjacent to our island may be found some of the best deep sea fishing in the world, and one of the most popular varieties is the famed Barracuda; there is good swimming the year round in the fresh-water of the rivers and in a crystal clear cool crater lake, or in the warmer, salt water of the coral-bottomed ocean.

Every division in camp owns a boat and many of the men have made excursions to adjacent islands where they trade tobacco, food and trinkets to the natives for seashells, model Outrigger canoes and ivory boar's tusks. And finally, with the recent installation on the base of a new ship's service store with a fountain, many of the boys go down and have a dish of ice cream and do a little reminiscing about the good old times spent at their favorite corner drugstore back in the "old country."

And say, you would really be surprised if you could see some of these banyan trees down here; an enormous bush-like tree which can't decide whether to make branches or roots. There is no end to the souvenirs of wood we can make from the mahogany, teak, and rosewood found here. And believe me, if my plans go through, I plan to bring or send home my share of these, too. Incidentally, since we are in the southern hemisphere, the trees and buildings throw their shadow from the sun or moon to the South, instead of, to the north as we were formerly accustomed.

The edible fruits are banana, coconut, papaya, (an oblong, yellow fruit which looks like a melon inside and is rich in vitamins), and of course, oranges and lemons. If you ever come to the tropics and want to try some coconuts, be sure and drink the milk from the green ones and eat the meat from the ripe ones. Take it from me, mate, I learned from experience!

There are huge bats, parakeets, and many varieties of varicolored birds which hold reveille for us every morning with all their singing and chattering in the jungle trees overhead. Also, some of the fellows have caught wild turkey, chicken, dove, and pig in the jungle. The most poisonous snake is the coral snake, but it does not bother you unless molested and fortunately is never seen out of the water.

Our quonset huts, which are screened at either end, are well off the ground, and with the protecting foliage, are very comfortable on the extremely hot, humid, summer days.

Well, there goes chow call and time for me to "knock off". Please don't forget to write, cause that sweet word is really appreciated at mail call.

Esther in a grass skirt

May 26, 1944

Author's note: Esther headed this letter with "Somewhere in the New Hebrides." She had moved on to Espiritu Santo, the main U.S. Naval Base in the South Pacific.

I sent a V-mail with my new address, so don't forget to change it when you're writing to me. You won't have to worry about me because I'm already here. It's a little rugged, at the present moment, as there are more than a dozen of us living in one long barracks—fun though.

I didn't get to buy a doll for Barbara before I left. Nancy should have hers by now, and you should have received the box I sent quite some time ago. Oh! Yes, before I go any further, Jean was here for a short time. I seem to be retracing his steps. I had a letter from him, and he is now going to school.

Do you know those anklets that you wear in shoes so that they don't show? It's to protect the shoes when you don't wear long hose or street anklets. Could you get me about half a dozen pair and send them to the above address?

I must apologize for not writing very much, but I'm rather tired tonight and I didn't want you to worry about me.

Have you heard from Wilber and Tiny lately? I hope they're both well and all the rest.

I have to do a washing tomorrow as my clothes are all dirty again. We had a very pleasant time coming out, but somehow your clothes really show the effect.

I must dress for chow as I am starved as usual and so until the next time, as they say.

June 1, 1944

I have your letters of May 6th, May 9th, May 16th, and May 13th before me. I had one waiting for me when I arrived, which really helped a lot.

Our quarters here are quonset huts with eight of us living together, quite a contrast to our former quarters but fun (Author's note: According to Naval Advance Base Espiritu Santo from Wikipedia, the floor space of the Quonset hut was 16 by 36 feet).

We just cracked a coconut and drank the juice. It has a very peculiar taste. The little lizards make themselves right at home in our house, and last night, we caught a rat. We use the farm style head—you know that type we had at home before you put in the indoors one? But it's fun.

I saw my former roommate Tony the other day and had lunch with her. She was in Frisco the same time we were awaiting orders. She's really black now and has a lovely suntan.

My mosquito bites that I got in New Caledonia have all disappeared. It didn't take long to get rid of them. I spent the whole morning washing. My trunks haven't arrived yet, and I brought only three uniforms with me so with the tablecloths, sheets, and pillowcases, I'll make a qualified laundress.

The beach is beautiful here. The water is so blue. We took a small boat and rode in on the waves. Gee! I wish you could see it all too. I haven't found many shells here, but I really haven't looked very well.

I'm glad that Tiny is still with Bill. I'll try and dash off a line to her someday, if I ever get my clothes clean.

I had a lovely letter from Jean too. He is really adorable, I only wish I could be with him now. I try to write frequently but I'm really not so good at it.

Tell all the kids hello. As soon as I catch up, I will try and write a longer letter. So, I must close and get to work.

Esther at the beach

June 7, 1944

I received your May 31st letter today, which is exactly seven days, and it was good to hear from you. As for the insurance, I've been paying it yearly but it's down quarterly. I hope I'm back by this time next year and then I can take care of it.

Did John Vern get a pony? I understand that John had bought a new horse, but it was too wild for John Vern to ride.

Will you please send me six pairs of peds? We wear no stockings with our uniforms, and I need them to wear in my shoes.

I had a letter from Leona today and she was talking about their experience the last day of school.

I'm going to try and get a letter off to Wilber tomorrow or the next day. I had a letter from Jean several days ago and he sounded so lonesome.

It is really interesting here. As I sit and write this, I can hear, a noise resembling monkeys chattering. I have seen the outline of them at night but never in the daytime. I'm told their faces resemble a fox and they have wings like a bat. The natives I understand make soup out of them (Author's note: It sounds like she's talking about tropical fruit bats found throughout the Pacific).

Along our coral walk to the mess hall, you can find several weeds and grass, but the peculiar one is the one that has leaves similar to a fern and when you touch or kick it, the leaves curl up. It has small purple flowers on it.

I am still without my trunks but getting along nicely except for a few things that I have to borrow which I hate.

We've been going to the beach almost every morning and my tan is slowly increasing. It is really lovely here. I hope to find enough shells to make some bracelets. Guess what? I received a grass skirt today—when I can get plenty. Bill promised me one back in February and it's been in the mail ever since March.

We had to leave Gasper behind again. I really miss her, because we had so much fun in New Zealand. As soon as Steve sends me a copy of those pictures, I will send you some. I really made him work.

I must say goodnight. Write soon and please send the peds as soon as possible.

Photo with a native islander

Letter to her sister Leonia (Nonie) Carson and family

June 10, 1944

I just received your letter telling about John Vern's last day of school. It was really some occasion and no wonder you'll never forget it. I have some New Zealand coins for him when I find out for sure whether I'm allowed to send them or not. As for the carbon copies, I know what you mean.

Did you ever receive the package I sent? I've just wondered if it ever arrived. You have never seen so many spiders as you do around here—when taking a shower, you can gaze up at the

ceiling and there you will find all sizes, shapes, et cetera, and
some of the most beautiful webs one could hope to see.

Everyone in our shack is either in bed or out, so I stay out in
our front room, which is beautiful. We painted the walls yellow,
used mosquito netting for curtains. Crettone drapes (green)
with green and buff wicker chairs. A telephone drum made into
a coffee table, a brown writing desk and the indispensable
ironing board.

Each girl has a cup of her own and one of the girls painted
the names on them in red. The cups are buff. The floor has red
wax on it. And a few coconuts with wires for vines. Quite cute
and we're really proud of it. I'm always afraid these are too hard
to read with my writing—no more room.

June 26, 1944

It really doesn't make any difference if the letters are of
carbon just as long as we hear from you. I sometimes feel that
I'm repeating myself and run out of things to say and then it's
stupid to write but I keep right on.

I received the cutest letter with a picture from Homer. I only
wish I had one in uniform to send him.

Things here are about the same. I have two days off after
two weeks of night duty, and woe is me, there is no plan except
to go swimming, dancing, boating and other minor things, but
it's the same people. I wish you were here to cut my hair. Before
long, I will resemble the natives, except for the color, and I do
believe it's changing too.

I've heard from Jean almost every day— he's going to school
now. I hope he has to stay there a while. I don't have to worry
as much then. Well, I just must start saying my adieus as the
bottom of the page is in sight.

Tell John Vern I'm glad he likes the horse, pony, or whatever it is.

~

Letter to her sister, Alberta Murphy and family

June 11, 1944

While waiting for the telephone to ring, I'll dash off a few lines. I have telephone watch from 0830 to 1200, and tonight, I go on night duty so if you don't hear from me for a while, consider the considerations. I finished dusting the place after the boys swabbed the deck so while they're talking, I dashed off a few lines.

It is rather nice here, but I imagine one would soon get tired of it. The coconuts at the present time are beautiful and they have a habit of falling almost any place, even on top of your head—what a life.

I should do a washing today, but weather doesn't permit so I'll just have to postpone it for the time being.

You should really see me I'm even washing my own uniforms. I didn't think I could ever do it but I'm managing beautifully. I decided if the boys could do it so could I—I've actually been washing my own sheets and pillowcases. Don't mistake it we have a washing machine and a mangle.

I had a letter from Homer Nauman. He sounded so homesick or rather he wanted to talk to someone from home.

I've seen a great deal of a man who flew here with us. He is an excellent dancer and fun to be with. He has promised to teach me to swim real well. I'm still afraid to get my head wet.

You probably already know about my change of address but just in case it's on the envelope. I received a letter from the folks today, and it arrived in eight days, allowing for the difference of time in our different places.

I spent one whole morning working in our flower garden. The wildflowers here are really beautiful. We painted our cabin, made some curtains out of mosquito netting, and it's simply precious. Golly my spelling is gradually getting worse. I must close. Everyone else is at church this morning—write when you find time.

Snapshot of Esther and friends sailing

June 16, 1944

Received your May 16th letter several days ago, also your April 15th. It was wonderful to hear from you. How I would love to see the kids. They really must be growing.

I had a letter from Nonie several days ago. Mail comes much faster here than at our former place.

I don't really care how you spell Frisco just as long as I hear from you. You see the letter went to the ward and the Phm.'s (Author's note: the abbreviation probably means pharmacist's mate) home was there, so he said as a result he told me about it. I just simply told him not to be nosey, because I was happy just as long as I heard from you.

I also had a letter from Homer again. We have really struck up quite a correspondence. He sent me his picture, so I suppose that was a subtle hint for me to send him one if I can find one.

Tonight will be my fifth night on night duty—isn't it wonderful? Since arriving here I don't know whether I'm coming or going.

Haven't heard from Jean for almost two weeks. I worry so much about him. He really is a swell person.

Your sewing is similar to mine. I always get in a hurry too or lose patience before I'm through.

This is really an interesting place, but you make your own fun. Does Bobby like shells? I'm trying to pick up enough for all three of the boys. I had a doll ordered for Barbara but apparently it hasn't arrived yet because they were sending it to me.

I now have the grass skirt that Bill promised me last February. It has been in the mail up until now. I'm going to have Steve send me some embroidery so I can do it. I intended to get some in New Zealand but never got around to it. I must close now. Write when you find time.

June 27, 1944

I received your June the 4th and June the 11th V-mail letters. Was it ever good to hear from you. Today seems like Christmas. I now have Barbara's doll and will send it off soon. I received a box from Edith Finney with cologne and panties and then a package with a photograph book and the little stickers for the pictures but no letters.

I'm going to try and write Wilber every week but by the time I get the folks and all the rest including Jean's answered, I'm sleepy. Golly! Has Nonie really been married ten years. It doesn't seem like it.

We at last have our trunks, and needless to say, it was wonderful. I was washing my own uniforms as I only had three in my suitcase. As for my birthday, we use slips, but I have plenty and if you wouldn't mind making it two bras size 32. I'd appreciate it. Gee! I'm really getting awful.

Lord, I forgot Wilber's birthday. I don't know what I could send him out here anyway but a letter. Jean has one too pretty soon.

You know I was a Godmother? Johnny's baby and I'll have to get him something in August. All I can think of is a bond. What do you think? This is grandma or can you buy cute things now? He will be two years old in August. I haven't met any of the kids from home as yet, and I must be getting old because a lot of the kids know Tiny.

I did a washing yesterday and all I would have had to do would be to hang it on the line. We go to the movies almost every night. I was going sailing today but the weather won't permit so I'll have to stay at home and iron.

Gee! All my envelopes have stuck together which makes me very unhappy. I must close and get to work.

Letters to her parents

July 7, 1944

Here it is July and it's really like spring, not too hot, not too cold. Needless to say, most everyone is enjoying it.

I have your letters of June 20th and 24th here, and it was swell to hear from you. Most of them, except the ones with the PEDs in, are coming through in eight or nine days. I usually forget we are always ahead of you.

I heard from Steve, Francis, Homer, Nonie, Bert, Johnny, Lois Bahr, and three from Jean. I'm sorry about the flowers and send very best wishes for your anniversary. I intend to send a money order to Dad as shopping on our rock is scarce. We have a few plantations, French and Australian, but most of them are native villages and all I can find are grass skirts. I don't think he would like one of those.

I wanted to ask for that gingham dress with the checks in it and my brown slacks. I might have given the dress away if so, don't bother with it. We wear sport clothes frequently to the beach and traveling in jeeps also. To save our white uniforms, we slip a dress on for lunch, breakfast, but for dinner. We always dress in either our ward uniforms or dress blues or whites—no hose on duty. They don't have any white nylon hose also, do they? And will you send a box from me for Wilber for Christmas? Put in some cartoons, etc. and a box of some kind. I know it's a little early but better early than never.

Tell Mrs. Bloom and everyone hello. One of our roommates just walked in with a letter from Bert.

I'm trying to listen to the radio and write at the same time. It's the news commentator, and it at least sounded more optimistic but there is a lot of static.

I really celebrated the 4th of July. We spent the whole day at the beach and took our lunch with us, and then in the evening, we went to the club for a dance. So, all in all it was a wonderful day. If someone accidentally stops by to see you think nothing of it.

I wish I could send you the pictures we took in New Zealand. The scenery at least is pretty. The other day while we were at the beach. We saw the largest land crab. They move rapidly sideways. They soon burrow into the sand and disappear from sight. We walked along the beach until we came to a freshwater stream. The foliage is tropical, and they have some very peculiar trees.

These particular trees had branches and from these, other branches grew to the ground and then would take root. As we were walking along, something hopped in front of us over the water. It clung to the side of the trees and when we chased it from the tree, it hopped along the sand. I'm not sure what it was but as somebody suggested tree fish, I took it for granted— end of page, so all for now.

Letters to her sister, Alberta Murphy and family

July 26,1944

I have your letters from June the 26th and July the 4th before me. It doesn't seem possible that it's time to combine wheat as this is supposedly the winter season here. I'm looking forward anxiously to the summer months.

One of my patients is making a frame for Tiny's wedding picture for me. I'm really happy about it—as yet my pictures are swell. I keep them in my hat locker and they very seldom mold.

I spent the morning washing and ironing, shining shoes, etcetera. It seems that I never get done.

I had two letters from Jean today, but they were both old ones. Gee! It would be good when I can see him.

I forgot about the folk's wedding anniversary. Did you all do anything? If so, do I owe someone something? I haven't mailed Barbara's doll, as yet, but I will as soon as I can. I don't think it's as pretty but it's more suitable for her age. Write soon.

August 5, 1944

I received your July 19th letter several days ago and am just getting around to answering it. I also received the letter with the pictures and the birthday package. Thank you ever so much for everything, including the writing in your letter.

Did Barbara ever receive her doll? Oh! Yes, your letters aren't censored so you didn't have to mark out where Cleo is stationed. She really looks like a pretty girl.

I'll be Esther for a while and give you my day. I was up at 0600 and dressed for duty by 0700 at which time I ate a hearty breakfast of toast, coffee, and fruit juice. They had some cereal and creamed ham for the toast, but I like mine plain.

At 0730 we were on our wards, this being Saturday and since I was on the morning shift, I only had to work until noon. I did my family washing and ironing in the afternoon, and since I talked myself out of going to the dance, I went to the movies, returned home, and mended my clothes. I was going to bed at 2100 but since it's 2400 now I'll never make it. Good night for now.

August 10, 1944

It's hard to realize that last year I was home at this time. Congratulations on your wedding anniversary and also your birthday. I'm sorry I have no cards, but my wishes are with you anyway.

I must tell you I've written everyone else about our heart of palm salad. It is obtained from the top of coconut trees when they are cut down. They say it is very expensive in the States and hard to get.

Bobby looks so much larger than all the kids. Isn't he big enough for a pony yet?

I had two letters from Jean again today. He has finished school and is at home for a few days when Lord only knows where he'll be assigned.

I don't know why I always pick the easterners to go with, but I do. I must sign off as I'm getting again to the bottom of the sheet—I for one hope this thing is over with soon.

Just returned from the beach where we had a wonderful swim and now, we're getting ready to go to the show. —Just returned from the show "Weird Woman." It had five women, and they all look weird to me. Had a lot of truth in it though—stories or opinions can be transmitted by a subtle suggestion from one person to another. The beach was also grand, but I've lost quite a bit of my suntan.

If you listen to the radio broadcast from K. F. B. I. service program in about 3 weeks, you will hear some of my patients. Their homes are all near Los Angeles.

Had a letter from Homer. He was so proud of the snapshot I sent him. He said it was the only one he had of me.

Whereabouts in Nebraska did the Haydens move to? I should remember, but I can't for the life of me.

Oh Yes! Enclosed is a money order for $10 for Father's Day—Now I'm a little late but I eventually get around.

If you by any chance don't hear from Jean for a while, think nothing of it. He has another ship the USS Metcalf, and so it takes letters some time to arrive.

I finally started to read as a pastime. Right now, I'm on the life of Gene Stratton Porter. It should be good.

Last night I was all caught up on my letter writing and tonight I have to start all over again—nothing new or different so I'll close for now. Hope you're all OK.

August 21, 1944

I've often wondered if you have any difficulty reading my V-mails. I realized the ink isn't very dark—just wondering.

It would be fun going to the Pla-Mor once again (Author's

note: an abbreviation for Play More, this was a neighborhood
club for playing games and socializing). Don't tell me Ralph and
I are the only ones not married. —Jeepers, is he waiting for me?
Nevertheless, you must still have fun. Do you play cards and
does Lavern always get high prize?

It seems our institutions have a tendency to promote gloom.

I attended a dance last night with the infant. He is the whole
sum of 23 but he looks 15. As a result, I have a crippled toe. He
didn't land on it though.

I'll still take Jean. He is really wonderful. I sometimes forget
that you haven't met him. I listen to the kids rave about how
handsome their boyfriends are and the pictures you should see.
I'll still take Jean.

Letters to her sister, Alberta Murphy and family

August 27,1944

I received your August 14th letter several days ago. I know
you'll all be glad to see Bill and Tiny.

It sounds wonderful to say you had supper in the basement.
We've had heart of palm salad several times which is really delicious, but it is at the very top of the tree. The palms as you can
tell by pictures are very hard to climb. Will you ask mother next
time you see her if she'll send me some 127 film?

I'm sorry to hear about Homer T. Is he going to divorce her?
Funniest feeling today. One of the patients looked something
like Jean. I know I was rude and stared, but I couldn't help it.
He is going to a ship that has the name of a former patient of
mine. I only hope our good luck continues, because I really
think a lot of him more so than anyone I've ever known except
Winston, and I know that couldn't be.

Had a letter from Steve she was over working as usual. So

long for now. Also had a letter from Aunt Anna and Uncle
Ernest, almost fainted.

～

Letters to her parents

September 4, 1944

I received a letter from you yesterday with the one enclosed
(copy) from Wilber. It was granted here that you were all well.

As usual I've been spending my spare time at the beach or
movies.

We had dinner at a place called Charley's. We ate outside in
an Arbor covered with vines. It was a lovely place as the stars
were shining above. Dinner was served in four courses. For the
first one, we had pork and a salad with potatoes and beets. The
salad had French dressing on it.

They removed the plates and placed another in front of us.
This time, an omelet with greens was served after which the
plates were removed and another one placed in front of us. This
time, steak with French fried potatoes was served. Again, the
plates were removed, and another placed in front of us, except
this time it was green, the others being white. We were served
cake and coffee. Also, a large glass of wine.

Tonight, we spent the evening before chow at the club for a
drink. Then after chow we went to the movies, and we were
fortunate enough to have a stage show which was excellent. We
also saw Jack Benny and Carol Landis about a week ago, But the
band tonight was wonderful.

I had my tetanus and typhoid shots today and as a result my
arm is a little sore. Must say good night now as I go to work in
the morning.

Letters to her sister, Alberta Murphy and family

September 13, 1944

I have your August 27th V-mail before me that I haven't answered. Is it the same dog that Bobby had before? The kids really must be growing. I sincerely hope I'm home before Christmas—not just wishful thinking. I've thought of resigning since Jean is in the States and will be for a few more months. I'm just waiting now.

Our life here has taken on a routine atmosphere. Although it's still nice. I was up at 0630, had breakfast at 0700 and to work at 0730. I was off at 1500. So, the rest of the day was mine to do with as I pleased. I'm trying to catch up on my letters, packing, and my blue skirt fell on my hot locker bulb, so I had to mend that—shine shoes and the ironing had to be done. I must close now.

September 30, 1944

I have your August 21st and September 18th letters before me. I was out of the letter writing mood as a result. I'm way behind.

Washington doesn't sound like the same place—by the way, Don Cameron told me that Viola's son was in the Navy—isn't he the one that was so ornery?

Why on earth don't you let Barbara play with the doll? I have some shells for the boys, but I'll send them to one and he can divide them. It sounds silly but it's easier on the post office and for me to pack. Oh! Yes, I have Barbara and Nancy's

Christmas present. You'll laugh your head off when you hear, none other than grass skirts (small size) I'm not sure that I can send them through the mail, so I'll probably have to bring them back.

Nancy Taddiken and Barbara Murphy in grass skirts sent from
Espiritu Santo, New Hebrides by their Aunt Esther Taddiken,
Easter 1945

Jean said that if he got priority, he would fly across country and stop and see you all. I do hope he makes it.

Do you know any Dotsons? People seem to have me confused with Lavonne (her sister aka Tiny). Oh yes! I had a letter from Jenny June. She seemed to be doing very well. I also had a letter from Homer and Johnny. She is at her folks near Manhattan.

We still spend a lot of time on the beach. It is so lovely there. Although my suntan isn't as brown as it was. I always feel off.

I almost finished this before chow, but didn't quite succeed so I will continue from there. It wasn't too bad, chicken soup (canned), orange salad, pork, beans and a resemblance of a

spice cake with jello. I have gained a little weight. I will close
now as I want to write several tonight.

Letter from Esther's brother, John Wilber, in the Army from his posting in Germany

October 5, 1944

Just finished reading my collection of letters from you.
There are six of them, written between June 24th and August
7th. Gosh, how my hospital mail is pouring in. I get from 10 to
15 letters every day, all old, and what a mess to keep straight.

Thanks a million for your picture, it's really good. I'd say you
are doing OK by the Navy. I sure envy you the climate you're in
now. Just now as I was sitting here in the Jeep reading your
descriptions of days spent on the beach and picnics, I began to
think of the weeks we spent on the beach in Sicily after the
campaign. Doggone if I didn't begin to feel warm for the first
time for quite a while, just thinking about it. What weather
we've had the past couple of weeks, wet, cold, and miserable.
Today we drew overshoes, gloves, overcoats, wool caps, and
another blanket. I'll probably turn warm now.

As you know we aren't very far inside Germany yet and
consequently haven't come in contact with very many German
people. However, the ones we have seen aren't so bad. Some
smile and wave, some look sore, but the biggest majority ignore
us. It's a lot different than the flag waving, flower throwing
French and Belgian people, but still better than we expected.

Say do you know how and when Jean was wounded? I never
did know. Mother writes that he is back out on a ship again.
What's the name of the town he's from? We have a couple of
fellows in the troop from Maryland.

Kind of tickles me when people write and say they're sorry to hear that I have malaria and hope that I'm soon out of the hospital. That's just backward from the way I look at it. I only had one chill after going to the hospital and as soon as my stomach settled down, I thoroughly enjoyed myself. Only one big drawback. Why do you people have to be so G.I.? Or are you in the Navy?

A fellow just out of combat finds it very hard to go around throwing "highballs" (Author's note: probably slang for saluting) and snapping to attention every time an officer happens his way. Maybe we expect too much, but to our way of thinking, all combat men deserve the right to relax and be at ease at least through their brief stay in a hospital. Sorry I haven't been able to write much. I'll try to do better from now on.

Letters to her sister, Alberta Murphy and family

October 26, 1944

I didn't know I was so far behind in answering your letters, but I found three of them tonight namely September 5th, October 2nd, and October 8th. Mail is taking much longer now so I haven't heard for several days.

Barbara sounds awfully cute—is she walking yet? I just wrapped the grass skirts yesterday, and I will have to have them censored before I can send them on. They're awfully cute.

I actually broke down and went to church a week ago Sunday. The sermon was very good. It is a long quonset hut. The altar is in the front and very attractive for this part of the country. I was going to choir practice (even with my voice) but in the meantime I developed a cold and as a result, I couldn't stop coughing long enough to carry a tune which I can't do anyway.

I had a letter from Jean about three days ago, and he's on his way to the West Coast. I do hope I get to see him soon. Have you heard from Tiny and Bill?

Letter to her sister, Leona (Nonie) Carson and family

October 26, 1944

I hope this finds you all well. I just dashed off a few lines to Bert, and I still have Jean to write to tonight. Time goes so swiftly out here that weeks pass before one realizes it.

I've been on PM duty the last two weeks. As a result, I go to the beach almost every morning. About eight of us start at 8:30 and stay until 11:00 o'clock which gets us back in time for a shower and lunch, and then if nothing comes up, we have time for a nap or cleaning the hut, washing, ironing, etc. That always has to be done.

Does Elaine like it where she's at? Gee! It's almost our curfew hour which is 11. We aren't allowed out after that.

I understand there is a Dodson boy here, but I haven't been able to get in touch with him. I've called several times, but it seems they have to take several hours looking it up. Must say so long.

Letters to her parents

November 19, 1944

Sorry I'm so late. I have your November 7th, September 26th, November 4th, October 28th, and October 31st letters before me. I received a letter from Bert saying you hadn't heard in three weeks—the truth is the island is running out of mater-

ial, and I'm so far behind in my correspondence, that I take one
look and give it up.

Thanks for the dress protectors and film. I really appreciated
them. I also received the Christmas package, and I must make a
confession I opened it, and I can sure use everything in it. It
doesn't seem possible that it can be so near the holiday seasons.
Time passes rapidly here. It could be the early hour that we
retire. I also received a package from Loretta Sullivan (nurses
training classmate), Francis Susan, and Aunt Anna and Uncle
Will. Yesterday I received a box of candy from Shanty for
Thanksgiving. It seems more like Christmas now.

I had a letter from Jean yesterday. I'm only afraid that he will
leave the States before I return, which I hope with all my heart
doesn't happen.

I spent the day yesterday cleaning our quonset hut. We
waxed the deck, swept down the spider webs, and as we have
no windows, we just brush the screens. Our garden needs
weeding, but we're waiting until a rainy day comes along.
After, the above mentioned things, we put on our play clothes
and retire to the beach. It was wonderful as usual. When we
returned, I still had the washing and ironing to do so I
speedily put that away and took my afternoon nap of 15
minutes. When I went off duty by 11 that night, I was ready to
hit my sack. Gee! I better stop the gibbering. Jean sends his
love.

November 26, 1944

I received a letter from you today and was happy to hear. As
yet I haven't heard from my resignation, but hope to soon. I
also received your October 29th letter with the hairnets.
Thanks ever so much. I just returned to the quarters from work

and found John Vern and Roger's picture. They really have grown.

Last night we spent the evening singing Christmas carols. It must be because everyone is receiving packages. I had one from Aunt Mayne and Aunt Anna. I opened them all. There was a beautiful, embroidered towel, butter knife, and some strawberry preserves. Also candy and nuts. I believe I told you about Francis and Loretta. Golly, my Christians will soon be over.

I sent the grass skirts and some shells to John Vern. There are some black ones with spots. I believe there's enough for one for each family.

I'm way behind in my correspondence which isn't unusual. Hope this finds you all well and not working too hard.

I guess you know our chicken got caught in the rat trap and was killed and the cat had five kittens.

Did you have a lovely Thanksgiving? I spent the day working until 1300 when I went swimming. We returned at about 1600 when I dressed, and we had dinner at the doctor's mess which was really delicious turkey and all the trimmings. In the evening, we attended a dance, and I must say I was ready for bed when we got back, but it was a lovely day.

I still haven't written you a story about a trip we took several weeks ago. Must close now.

Letters to her sister, Alberta Murphy and family

November 27, 1944

I have several of your letters here, but I forgot my box so I can't give you all of the dates. I would love to see Barbara and Bobby. They must be awfully cute. I suppose Barbara has grown a lot.

Christmas packages have been arriving, and it seems more

like Christmas now than it probably will then. The sweetest
thing happened. A patient wrote and had his mother send me
some chicken (canned). As a result today I received a package
with a can of chicken and fruit cake. And on top of that, a very
good friend of mine received a box from home with fudge cookies, nut rolls, and fruit cake so he brought that over—our hut is
actually getting fat. Thanksgiving he brought over some
eggnog, tomatoes, and a pineapple. The latter two he grew in
his own garden. There were also dates and some more fruit
cake. Just a few more pounds.

I've really met some interesting people since coming out
here. As yet, I haven't heard from my resignation. Here's hoping
that I soon have some word. I've heard from Jean frequently
lately, and I hope he's still there when I get back. Jean's mother
is making me a large doll out of yarn I believe. She really must
be sweet.

I sent the grass skirts to mother, and she'll give them to the
girls. Just hang them out in the sun before you put them on. I
went shopping the other day—army PX—I came back with a
seersucker dress, raincoat, two pairs beige hose, one pair (dirty
green) anklets. Not bad.

I do hope you had a nice Thanksgiving. I really had a swell
one. Must close now.

December 18, 1944 from Honolulu, Hawaii

Yes, I'm in this far. I don't know when I'll complete the trip,
but I hope soon.

I've had a lovely trip so far. Gee! I wish you'd all been with
me. I didn't think it would happen to me.

It's lovely here as far as I've seen, and I've met so many old
acquaintances. Just like homecoming.

Have you heard from Wilber yet? I suppose he's still hard at it.

News is scarce and I'm rather tired. Traveling is wonderful after a fashion, but you always have to keep your clothes clean, shoes shined, etcetera.

I wish you could hear the music over the radio. Just like home. It seems so funny at first, but I guess I'll get used to it.

Everyone has been so wonderful here. We even have a glass of fresh milk which tasted powerful good (it wasn't canned) and potatoes that tasted like something besides mush. I forgot to have you send Jean a Christmas box. I hope you did though. Must close now.

~

December 20, 1944 from Honolulu, Hawaii

Well, here I still am. I did so want to be with Jean for Christmas. Hope this finds you all well. Have you heard from Wilber lately?

I sent two packages today. Will you open them and save them for me please? If you don't open them, they'll curl, and I don't want that.

At the present moment, I have another cold which has kept me away from the beach, and besides, I hate to wash clothes.

I've been reading a book on the history of the place which is really interesting.

Oh! Yes, my trunks are on their way, and you'll receive no more checks for a while. I also gave my address there to the kids, so you'll get my mail.

How's Tiny and where is she going to work? Well, guess I'd better finish cleaning up the house as I'm not going to bed for a while yet.

RETURNING TO THE U.S

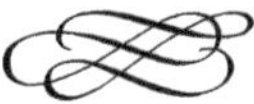

Esther resigned her commission in the Navy on November 2nd, 1944. The reason given in her resignation letter was matrimony.

Esther and Jean, February 2, 1945

After leaving Espiritu Santo on her way back to the continental U.S., Esther flew to Canton (Kanton) Island, the largest and northernmost island of the Phoenix Islands, in the Republic of Kiribati. Canton is roughly halfway between Hawaii and Fiji. She stopped at another Pacific island, Palymra, before reaching San Diego, California.

She was granted 71 days paid leave from December 28th, 1944, to March 8th, 1945. Her resignation would be effective March 8th, 1945.

Esther and Jean were married in Seattle, Washington on February 2nd, 1945.

REMINISCENCES

The following are things I remember Mom talking about during my childhood about her time in the military.

She collected shells from the beach to take home with her. Unfortunately, the shells were still occupied, and she had to deal with a stinky mess when she unpacked.

Something similar happened to me when I was in Australia at Cairns near the Great Barrier Reef. I picked up two shells I thought were empty on the beach and put them on the table in my hotel room. The next morning—much to my surprise—they started walking across the table. I took them back to the ocean where they belonged.

Mom said the most badly injured patients she had to deal with were the ones with shark bites. She mentioned them in her letters home from Mare Island Naval Base Hospital.

She always said that the Army nurses had it much harder than the Navy nurses. I found the account online of an Army nurse from Maine, who served in New Caledonia and the New Hebrides, "Veteran's Testimony—Lena R. Gelott, Army nurse, 48th Station Hospital." From Lena's account and the picture of her by her tent in the jungle, I would agree with Mom's assessment.

Mom was a fan of the book, <u>Back to Bataan,</u> and mentions it in her letters home. Eleven Navy nurses, 66 Army nurses and one nurse-anesthetist were taken prisoner by the Japanese when Bataan and Corregidor in the Philippines fell. They remained a nursing unit under very harsh conditions until they were liberated in February 1945.

Mom always talked about how well the Navy corpsmen performed their jobs. She mentions them frequently in her letters home. I did not understand the function of the corpsmen in relation to the nurses until I read "White Task Force," a Navy publication, NAVMED 939, published in 1945 on the history of the Navy Nurse Corps. The Navy Nurses trained the corpsmen to be nurses to care for the wounded on the battlefield. Basically, they were male nurses. Esther mentions caring for former colleagues as patients in her letters home. I would imagine she was talking about caring for wounded corpsmen she had trained or worked with.

She said she would have been promoted if she'd been able to type. One of her assignments, when she was at Mare Island Naval Base hospital, was in the front office. She sent a letter she had typed to her parents, and it was full of mistakes. I don't think office work was a thing my mother enjoyed. It's surprising that her skills as a nurse would not be a consideration for promotion.

WWII MEDALS

Mom was awarded for her military service:

- The World War II medal for participation in World War II from 1941-1945.
- The Asiatic Pacific Campaign medal for service from 1941-1943.
- The American Campaign medal for service from 1941-1945.

THE WHITE TASK FORCE, THE STORY OF THE NURSE CORPS UNITED STATES NAVY

The "White Task Force" was a publication, NAVMED 939, of the Bureau of Medicine and Surgery, United States Navy, published in 1945 by the U.S. Government Printing Office. One thing in this publication that was surprising to me is that the Navy Nurse Corps was only thirty-seven years old in 1945. It only dated from the first World War. I have excerpted significant portions of this publication relating to my mother's story.

The Nurse's Corps was established as a unit of the Navy in 1908. Nurses were assigned to the Naval Medical School Hospital in

Washington, D.C. The group consisted of a superintendent, a chief nurse, and 18 nurses. As the Navy did not provide quarters for these nurses, it was necessary for them to rent a house and open their own mess.

The introductory paragraph in this publication stated:

"From the time of Pearl Harbor, when the first enemy gun against our country was fired in World War II, until the last signatures dried on the peace documents in Tokyo Bay, Japan, Navy Nurses were with the fleet caring for its men. Through the smoke and fire and ruin of Pearl Harbor, they worked heroically to save lives without thought of their own safety, as well as through the succeeding long months of combat, wherever they were needed. At the war's dramatic end, they were with the fleet at the gates of Tokyo in several large hospital ships, to care for any emergencies which occurred and to take off United States prisoners of war from Japan.

Then came the aftermath—the weeks and months of healing those wounds of body and mind sustained by the fighting men—just as in the years and the wars before. Down through times' unfailing past have Navy nurses proven themselves equal to their own inceptors' fondest hopes."

General Quarters

In a section of the "White Task Force" titled General Quarters, came this statement and subsequent paragraphs:

> All American nurses are honored by the fact that theirs is the only woman's profession that the country deemed so essential as to be placed under the War Manpower Commission to ensure the maximum utilization of their abilities during the war.

In 1939, shortly before the storm broke over Europe, the U.S. began to awaken to its danger. Some fanatical opposition still flared, but all military services fought for public support in the preparation for the trials to come. Mobilization began. Selective service began to operate. The Navy recruited men and officers and began an intensive training program.

Through the period of retrenchment, there had been no enrollment of nurses into the Reserve Corps. In 1939, under authority of the Naval Reserve Act, qualified nurses began to be recruited for the Reserve Nurse Corps, to be ready immediately for active duty in the event of a national emergency.

All through the war, thousands of Reserve Nurses served beside the members of the Regular Corps all over the world. On July 31st, 1945, a fortnight before the surrender of Japan, the grand total of nurses was 11,021; 1,799 of whom were in the Regular Corps and 9,222 in the Reserve.

In spite of acute shortages throughout the country, the Navy was still able to hold to its standards and enroll nurses of outstanding qualifications and experience. In the Nurse Corps, they have found opportunities for the exercise of all their special abilities and skills.

Thousands of young men of the Navy had to be trained during the war to be hospital corpsmen. The majority of these hospital apprentices and pharmacists' mates had never been inside a hospital before their enlistment. Their teaching and supervision were important duties of the Navy Nurses, many of whom were experienced instructors with degrees and other teachings credentials.

Their contribution to this work was invaluable. Navy nurses were proud of the record of these men who tended our naval and maritime casualties aboard fighting ships and on invasion beaches, where nurses were not assigned.

Battle Stations

In a section of "White Task Force" called Battle Stations, the beginning praises the Navy Nurse's professional training. It goes on to say that in World War II, especially did nurses come into their own.

In the Pacific, Navy Nurses were the first American women to be sent to the islands north of New Caledonia, the first group going to Efate, in the New Hebrides. There they cared for the wounded from the long Guadalcanal campaign, Army as well as Navy and Marine personnel. Others were stationed in New Caledonia, the Solomon's, the Russells, New Zealand, Australia, New Guinea, and Hawaii. In these strange and famous places—the Coral Sea, Savo, Tarawa, Attu, Adak, Dutch Harbor, Kwajalein, Saipan, Tinian, Leyte, Samar, Iwo Jima, and Okinawa—Navy nurses kept their rendezvous.

In Oran (Per Wikipedia: The Battle of Oran, was part of Operation Torch, the Allied invasion of Algeria). In England and Italy, they cared for our men who won victory from the Nazis.

Aboard hospital ships, Navy Nurses followed the fleet in its thrilling assaults, going into the beaches with the fighting men to pick up the wounded and carry them back to base hospitals.

Salute

Another part of the "White Task Force" called Salute, dealt with the status and remuneration of Navy Nurses. With the great expansion and multiplication of duties of the Nurses of the Navy, new recognition came to the Corps. On July 3rd, 1942, an act of Congress granted nurses permanent relative rank of commissioned officers.

Corresponding base pay and, with some exceptions, allowances, were legislated December 22nd, 1942. With that legislation, Navy Nurses did not receive rental and subsistence and travel allowances for their dependents, but this was corrected in a bill passed by Congress effective October the first, 1944. On February 22nd, 1944, Congress provided that Navy Nurses during the present war and for six months thereafter should have actual commissioned rank.

Although members of the Corps always received the courtesies and enjoyed many of the privileges of officers of the Navy, the new recognition brought them honor and dignity, as well as increased authority consistent with the degree of responsibility which they carried. When war broke, all who thought seriously realized the necessity of providing the same protection to nurses serving in dangerous areas all over the world as is provided for doctors, dentists, and chaplains, with whom their work is so closely joined.

Esther and Jean were married in Seattle, Washington in February of 1945 after my father was mustered out of the Navy. They both said they thought long and hard about staying in California. However, Mom talked Dad into moving back to Maryland where he was born and raised.

They wound up in Annapolis after Dad got a job at the Naval Research and Development Center across the Severn River from the US Naval Academy. They bought a house in Pines on the Severn, Arnold, Maryland in 1948. It was right after the war and housing was scarce. The house they bought was originally a summer cottage for people from Baltimore. Mom said it was a good thing it was a mild winter or we would have frozen to death.

Mom volunteered as a nurse for public health distributing the polio vaccine. She volunteered in the health room at Severna Park High School and the Arnold Senior Center. She took care of my father's parents and her parents, as well as my father's uncle. Esther and Jean traveled to Kansas, California, Florida, Hawaii, Maine, and Canada.

In 1978, Mom took a merchant ship as a passenger with other Navy families to Central and South America in 1978. This was something she'd always wanted to do. She also took many courses at the Arnold Senior Center given by former state department personnel. During the course work, she visited many foreign embassies in Washington D.C.

Although Mom was eligible to be buried at Arlington National Cemetery, she chose instead to be buried at the Maryland State Veteran's Cemetery in Crownsville, Maryland. The Crownsville Cemetery is beautiful. The back wall of the small stone chapel is open to a view of rolling hills.

The flag presented at Esther's funeral with medals.

The cemetery also has a carillon that rings out on holidays. Mom, as a Naval officer, has her own grave. My father is buried next to her. Esther's grave is in Area 6, Section D-1, Row 10, Grave 10. Spouses of veterans are usually buried in the same grave.

My parents were older than my friend's parents because of their participation in World War II. My mother encouraged me to take advantage of every experience I could. I am very grateful for the support of both parents when I was growing up. I love them and miss them every day.

Mom was very humble and rarely discussed the war or her part in it. I was amazed to learn about the very important people she met and the experiences she had.

I am donating her letters from World War II, her papers, and the artifacts made by her patients to the Clay County Museum in her hometown of Clay Center, Kansas.